WHAT WOULD YOUR
CHARACTER DO?

WHAT WOULD YOUR
CHARACTER DO?

Personality Quizzes
for Analyzing Your Characters

Eric Maisel, Ph.D.
and Ann Maisel

WRITER'S DIGEST BOOKS
Cincinnati, Ohio
www.writersdigest.com

Distributed in Canada by Fraser Direct, 100 Armstrong Avenue, Georgetown, ON, Canada L7G 5S4, Tel: (905) 877-4411. Distributed in the U.K. and Europe by David & Charles, Brunel House, Newton Abbot, Devon, TQ12 4PU, England, Tel: (+44) 1626 323200, Fax: (+44) 1626 323319, E-mail: mail@davidandcharles.co.uk. Distributed in Australia by Capricorn Link, P.O. Box 704, Windsor, NSW 2756 Australia, Tel: (02) 4577-3555.

Visit our Web site at www.writersdigest.com for information on more resources for writers.

To receive a free weekly e-mail newsletter delivering tips and updates about writing and about Writer's Digest products, register directly at our Web site at http://newsletters.fwpublications.com.

10 09 08 07 06   5 4 3 2 1

Library of Congress Cataloging-in-Publication Data
Maisel, Eric
  What would your character do? : personality quizzes for analyzing your characters / Eric Maisel, Ann Maisel.
      p. cm.
  Includes index.
  ISBN-13: 978-1-58297-372-2 (pbk.: alk. paper)
  ISBN-10: 1-58297-372-5 (pbk.: alk. paper)
  ISBN-13: 978-1-58297-371-5 (hardcover: alk. paper)
  ISBN-10: 1-58297-371-7 (hardcover: alk. paper)
  1. Fiction--Technique. 2. Characters and characteristics in literature. I. Maisel, Ann II. Title.
  PN3383.C4 M35
  808.3'97--dc22   2006001398

• •

Edited by KELLY NICKELL
Designed by GRACE RING
Production coordinated by ROBIN RICHIE

■■■■■■■■■■■■■■■■■■■■■■■■■■■■

TABLE OF CONTENTS

■■■■■■■■■■■■■■■■■■■■■■■■■■■■

Your character spends several hours at a family picnic attended by parents,
grandparents, siblings, aunts and uncles, and other members of her extended family. Does she enjoy the event or spend it hiding in the bathroom?

Your character is called to jury duty for a criminal case such as a rape
charge or, alternatively, for a civil case involving product liability.
Does he embrace his civic responsibility or try to shirk it?

Your character is on vacation and, while sunning herself by the pool,
has an encounter with a stranger who asks a too-intimate question.
How does she respond?

THE IMPORTANCE OF
KNOWING YOUR CHARACTERS

CHAPTER NO. I
WHAT IS PERSONALITY?

Personality and character are the province of every thinking person but the special province of the psychologist and the writer. Psychologists—that is, clinical psychologists, psychiatrists, academic researchers in social psychology and developmental psychology, family therapists, clinical social workers, and so on—have a way of looking at personality and character that is determined in large part by the culture and constraints of their profession. The writer, too, is constrained to look at personality and character in ways that fit his needs, in his case the needs of fiction. Whatever psychologists and writers *really* think about personality, when they enter the consulting room or the writing study they enter a world of artifice.

Before I invite us into the writer's artificial world and explain what character means to a writer, I want to guide us on a journey into the psychologist's artificial world. The reasons for this excursion may not be apparent at first glance, but they will become clear as we proceed. Let me provide the headline now: Fiction writers have a leg up on psychologists when it comes to understanding personality and character. To put it differently: Fiction writers are our real psychologists.

Traditional Psychology

For thousands of years, natural philosophers and poets speculated about man's nature. In the late nineteenth century, a pair of historical events—Sigmund Freud's creation of psychoanalysis (a way of working therapeutically with people) and the trend in American psychology toward experimentation and instrumentation—led to the widely held belief that psychology was growing into a science. Since psychology had become, or was becoming, a science, it seemed logical to presume one of its goals would be to produce a scientific theory of personality, exactly like the theories of planetary motion or gas expansion. Such a theory would fully and accurately explain how human beings tick.

This goal, although more implicit than explicit, drove early psychologists to create theories of personality that claimed to pinpoint the central mechanisms of personality. They invented the language of this territory as they went, introducing words like *unconscious*, *regression*, *ego*, *archetype*, and scores of other words meant to stand for concepts that they claimed were real but that, in retrospect, they were only positing. Nobody could really say what a word like *ego* represented—though clinicians intuitively felt they could distinguish between, for example, someone with high ego strength and someone with low ego strength. Could they really?

Perhaps they could or perhaps they were really sensing a difference in *glock* or *wang*, or some other quality that no one had successfully articulated, operationally defined (a necessity in science), run experiments on, or nailed down. Maybe there weren't any qualities of the sort they were positing. Maybe they had missed the boat entirely and, like the Sufis in the myth, were mistaking the trunk, the tail, or the hide for the elephant. Certainly nobody examining the theories they created came away with the impression that human beings as we knew them, with inner lives, imaginations, and the occasional wry smile and outburst of pique, were being portrayed.

Still, clinicians held to their impressions and their favorite theories, and classes in theories of personality sprang up in universities everywhere. These classes did not represent what you would expect a class with such a title to represent, namely a coherent investigation of clearly distinguishable theories leading to a winner or at least a favorite. Rather, they tended to provide a cursory rundown of the famous names in psychology—Freud, Carl Gustav Jung, Alfred Adler, Karen Horney, George Kelly, Erik Erikson, mostly names from the early part of the twentieth century—and their major ideas. This lack of rigor and this lack of a winner—this lack of even the criteria by which a winner might be determined—further supported the skeptic's contention that some individual's random impressions had somehow gotten elevated to the rank of theory.

The fact that psychologists were not actually getting any closer to a solid, agreed-upon theory of personality, nor even getting closer to answering the question of whether such a hunt made any sense, might not have affected you and me very much. But it did. This failure had profound consequences for all of us. As a consequence of not having arrived at the facts of what makes us tick, no psychologist, psychiatrist, family therapist, or clinical social worker could say, except as a guess, what caused depression, anxiety, addiction, psychosis, or any of the other ailments that befall people. They were at a loss. Since nature abhors this sort of vacuum, pharmaceutical companies leaped in and began concocting compounds to fill the vacuum.

In the absence of a robust theory of personality, one that actually explained why a person might be anxious, depressed, addicted, and so on, mental health professionals were left with three ways of dealing with our emotional health. They could medicate you. They could rely on their clinical methods—say, the methods of psychoanalysis, for example, free association and working through transference—and stick with their methods whether or not they got positive results. Or they could do what natural philosophers had done for thousands of years, use their common sense and their understanding of human nature—and a lot of wit and warmth—to affect behavior change.

You could present this last sort of helping professional with any sort of human issue, and he would have a way of grasping the matter. Not having divided the universe into well and ill or ordered and disordered and construing human nature as an entanglement of causes, customs, and motivations, a tapestry of genetics and culture, he would smile, commiserate, chide, advise, listen, and even cry. He would make suggestions, not because he had a theory but because he had some ideas about what might help. There turned out to be all the difference in the world between standing behind a theory and having insights into human nature. The first could only be called pseudo-science; the second, wisdom.

Wisdom, however, was not much rewarded in a climate where clinicians needed to explain themselves to insurance companies, and graduate students needed to carve out their small niche as part of their journey toward a doctorate. The net result of a century of professional and academic psychology was the widespread wonder as to what clinicians and academics actually knew and to what extent they could actually help. When a given clinician did manage to help, the source of his healing power seemed to reside in his common sense, wisdom, humanity, and poetry, and not in anything that a hundred years of psychology had taught.

The Clinician and the Experimenter

The half-hearted attempts to construct an accurate theory of personality did not bear fruit, but they did lead to an array of results, many of them rather negative. On the negative side, there arose a clandestine pact among the players in the game to act as if they knew more than they did. Groups of players, formed into panels, were given the following assignment:

> Collect symptoms—insomnia here, a felt lack of pleasure there—and give your collection a name like "depression." Make sure not to hint at where this "depression" comes from, as we know nothing about that. Make the symptom list quite long and then randomly pick a number, not too large, so that we can tell practitioners something like, "If you see five of these eleven symptoms, any five, you can call the person depressed—and you can bill his insurance company." Okay? Get going!

In such a way did the *Diagnostic and Statistical Manual of the American Psychiatric Association* come into being. It is now universally used by clinicians to *diagnose*, although the players in the game know (or ought to know) that this is such a funny way to go about diagnosing as to deserve its own Monty Python skit or National Lampoon movie. In medicine, evidence is employed to help a clinician know what is causing the symptom. In the mental health world, evidence cannot be employed that way because causation is not on the table. It is as if a doctor were to say to you, "Yes, that is a very big lump on your neck, so we're going to say that you have lumpitis. Now, let's talk about your mother."

Because the fact that so little was actually known and what was known was being swept under the rug, no discipline-wide conversation about certain fundamental ideas could ever commence. Psychologists could not get on the table questions like "What do we presume is normal behavior?" or "What do we presume is a healthy personality?" "Normal behavior" meant little more than "stopping abnormal behavior," and "healthy personality" meant little more than "an absence of symptoms and their related symptom pictures." Today, if you ask a clinician what he presumes is normal behavior or mental health, his usual response is, "Well, that's hard to say, but Freud's summation is probably still the best: to love and to work. If you can love and if you can find a niche in the job market, you are healthy and normal."

While clinicians were colluding in glossing over the fact that human beings remained quite mysterious to them, experimenters set themselves a different agenda. They tried to do science or, let us say, modest science, as it proved much too difficult to do robust science with human beings as the experimental subject. Research psychologists found themselves repeatedly stuck at the same point. They would name a trait or quality that they intended to investigate—say, intelligence—construct a way of investigating that trait or quality—say, an intelligence test—run the test, consider the results, employ ideas from science like reliability and validity, and arrive at conclusions. All well and good—if they were ever measuring intelligence.

Because a given intelligence test might well be more measuring the cultural acquisition of language or manual dexterity, for instance, than intelligence, a score of 110 simply did not mean what the experimenter claimed that it meant. This is a significant problem—a grave problem, really. Much of experimental psychology suffered from this basic flaw, that after all the science was done, and even if it was done well, you didn't know what you had. Because you didn't know what you had, you didn't know what to recommend or do next.

For this central reason, that experimental psychologists couldn't really say what they were measuring when they went about doing their measurements, the majority of experiments in intelligence, motivation, emotion, learning, and other subjects of interest to researchers produced a welter of data but few insights into human nature. Still, some of their experiments produced eye-popping results that actually taught us something about our species. Psychologist Harry F. Harlow's attachment research (using monkeys) taught us volumes about the problems that arise in the absence of parental love and bonding. Social psychologist Stanley Milgram's obedience experiments, the most revealing experiments ever run, scared us to death about the average person's capacity for sadism and casual cruelty. Wonderful experiments like these shone like pearls.

But even these excellent experiments did not produce the result, perhaps impossible to achieve, of leading us any closer to a clear, comprehensive theory of personality. It was as if we were in a vast, dark basement and each new experiment shed light on some corner of the basement, but we remained with no way to turn on the overhead light and really see what the basement contained. So, these excellent experiments notwithstanding, an objective observer could only conclude that the experts had not provided us with anything like a road map to personality. If, that is to say, these *were* the experts.

The Writer as Experimental Psychologist

Why bring up the failings of professional psychology? I bring them up so that you, as a writer, do not feel that you have to play second fiddle to putative experts. There is no one more expert about the psychology of personality than you. The ordinary clinician opens his bible, the *Diagnostic and Statistical Manual of the American Psychiatric Association*, and names your problem according to the symptoms you report. If you report that you've been feeling blue for a certain number of days, have had trouble sleeping, and experience little or no pleasure from life, a clinician runs his finger down the page, looks up, and says it's major depression. A writer does something very different.

A writer gets inside his sleepless, blue character and discovers that she is blue because she has contrived a loveless marriage that made sense from one point of view, the security angle, but was a horrible mistake from the purely human angle, since her husband is a cipher. A clinician says it's major depression. A writer says, "Hmm. Given this inner conflict, given that she really does love her walk-in closet but hates her husband, what is she going to do? What if I bring in, not a handsome stranger, but someone she'd never look at twice under ordinary circumstances but who, by virtue of the fact that she is so conflicted, begins to attract her in an obsessional way? Wouldn't that be interesting?"

A writer sets up his own amazing experiment: his work of fiction. He says to himself, "How would a guilty conscience play itself out in a character who thinks that he is entitled to murder but discovers that he doesn't feel all that entitled?" The writer runs his experiment: He writes *Crime and Punishment*. He may think that he knows how his novel must end but he must still write the novel—run the experiment, as it were—to know for sure. Until he inhabits the landscape he has decided to investigate, he can't be certain that his characters are going to do what, at the moment of inception, he supposes that they must do. The novelist writes and, as he writes, he says to himself, "I know that Raskolnikov will ultimately confess, but I can't have him confess unless I get him there legitimately." The psychological legitimacy of the journey is the writer's paramount concern.

Whether we are reading genre fiction, literature, or even biography or memoir, we want the author to have gotten inside his characters and gotten us to the end of the piece legitimately. It is that effort at legitimacy, tested by the author and the reader in every paragraph, that we respect. It is the success-ful maintenance of psychological plausibility that we applaud. We don't need our authors to create indefensible theories of personality. We need them to do something more remarkable: We need them to understand personality.

It has proved too difficult and perhaps even downright impossible to create anything like a comprehensive theory of personality. We can't say with any certainty even the simplest things, for instance, whether depres-sion is a disease, a meaningful problem, a habit, or a choice. Yet we feel confident that personality shines through, that Uncle Max is a certain kind of person who consistently yells before he reasons, prefers football to polo, cheats on Aunt Mabel but not on Sundays when she makes her famous pot roast, and so on. We know or think we know Uncle Max. Might he have some surprising secrets or odd behaviors about which we aren't aware? Of course—but we don't think that changes the picture much.

Or does it? That question is so interesting to a writer! What if I told you that Uncle Max writes poetry? That Aunt Mabel started having affairs first? That while he watches football, Uncle Max is really thinking about sailing around the world? That his father beat him? That he has a pen pal in Egypt? That he keeps a box of Depends in the pickup because he sometimes has accidents? Would any of that change the picture? Would you still feel sanguine in saying that you *knew* Uncle Max or that Uncle Max was the same person that he appeared to be before you learned that information? Don't your writer glands just salivate at the prospect of making sense of these new incarnations of Max?

We are at a loss to know even what is *too* inconceivable in the realm of personality. Is it inconceivable that the strongest personality might crack under pressure? No. Is it inconceivable that a happy marriage of twenty-five years might flounder in the twenty-sixth year? No. Is it inconceivable that out of the clear, blue sky, just because a stray thought entered awareness, a person might change his career, his country, or his basic attitude toward life? No. In the realm of personality, it is hard to conceive of an inconceivable scenario. At the same time, we believe in the essential consistency of personality, such that if Uncle Max said something out of character we would know it.

This is the beautiful seemingly paradoxical place that we end our first dis-cussion about personality and character. The writer, the true expert on human nature, can contrive anything in the realm of human behavior. But whatever she contrives, she must still meet certain tests of plausibility and legitimacy.

CHAPTER NO. 2

UNDERSTANDING YOUR CHARACTERS

Is it possible to know what the characters in the novel you're writing would be likely to do if they found themselves empaneled on a jury, caught in a big lie, or entrusted with a deathbed secret? The answer is yes—and all the more so because they *are* fictional characters. Because of the way the mind invites in characters, as streamlined idea packages with a useful but simplified range of possibility, a writer actually knows her characters better than she knows the real people in her life, including herself. This may seem strange at first glance but should feel less strange as you ponder the matter.

Franz Kafka had considerable trouble understanding his own motives and the contours of his personality, but he knew exactly how Joseph K. would react to each new absurd defeat on his inexorable journey to punishment in *The Trial*. Kafka knew every nuance of Joseph K.'s personality because Kafka had in mind a kind of template that limited Joseph K. to a certain range of emotional and intellectual motion. Kafka might not have known how he himself would have handled a visit from his autocratic father but he knew perfectly how Joseph K. would react to such a visit.

A real person like your sister may have had a binge drinking period, a sober period, a thin period, a fat period, a promiscuous period, a celibate period, a time when she hated her mate, a time when she made peace with her mate, and so on. It isn't that your sister may not also exhibit a real consistency: Indeed, you may know exactly how she's going to react if you mention your father's profligate ways (angrily) or your brother's current antics (with wry amusement). But she is too human to pigeonhole perfectly, too regularly surprising in her inconsistencies, and, most importantly, not embedded in a fiction that constrains her.

Not caught up in a drama set in motion by word one and completed at word seventy-five thousand, your sister is simply freer than anyone in your novel. The characters in your novel are not people; they are fictional creatures who have come alive to serve your needs. They may demonstrate free will, because you construct them that way, but they do not possess free will. The necessarily simple consistency of a fictional character is not a problem to be remedied or a flaw that puts the power of fiction in doubt. It is simply an aspect of art.

This doesn't mean that fictional characters don't feel rich and real. By virtue of their very consistency, they partake of archetypal and stereotypical resonances and transcend the messiness of personality. A real person might change moods thirty-three times in a week. A character can't do such a thing without looking manic-depressive. A real person might harbor a secret nasty desire that in no way affects his goodness or reliability. A character may not, because as soon as we hear about that nasty desire we presume that it reflects on his character. A real person may act cowardly here and heroic there, but a character that acted that way would confuse and disturb us. The author leaves out the messiness and complexity of personality and by doing so creates memorable characters.

No character ever written is as complex as the least complex human being. Conversely, few actual human beings are as memorable as even the least interesting fictional character. Characters in a novel resonate because of their archetypal richness, their functional interrelationships, and the dynamics put into motion by the author, and not because they are as complex as real people are. This means that you, as the architect of your novel, can inhabit and understand your characters in a way that you could never understand the eleven strangers you join on a jury or the extended family of your in-laws whom you meet for the first time at a party. Those eleven strangers are really quite a mysterious lot but *your* twelve jurors, should you write that kind of novel, can be exactly what you need them to be.

Characters possess a necessarily limited range of motion. Still, they must be free enough to surprise you and engage you. On the one hand, because you have brought them to life and know a great deal about them, you probably have a very good sense of how your hero and heroine will react when they have their first fight. On the other hand, because you only know a great deal about them and not everything, you can't know for sure how their first squabble will unfold. You therefore arrive at that situation with a certain expectancy and openness to discovery and you allow your characters to just be. They are constrained by your themes and your ideas, but they are at least *this* free, that, for instance, you are surprised to find your heroine using her nails and your hero cursing.

It is no paradox that characters in a novel have limited freedom and acres of freedom. Because they serve the novelist's needs, they must not break out of the frame, like a cartoon character leaping out from the television screen and taking up residence in your guest room. In this sense, they must take orders. At the same time, they must be free to play out their personality and destiny, however constrained that personality and however preordained that destiny. Oedipus had no real choice about where he was heading, nor did Hamlet, nor did Ahab. But the author still had to get Oedipus, Hamlet, or Ahab to his preordained destination *legitimately*, through something that at least mimics freedom.

What this means is that it is in your power to know your characters quite well, if not perfectly or completely, and in your power to roughly predict how they are likely to act in various situations. You know them this well because you've invited them into your mind *as* certain kinds of characters. You will know them better, however, as you put them through their paces and drop them into various situations. The premise of this book is that the more situations you provide for your characters to experience, including situations that have nothing to do with your novel, the better you will understand them. We'll return to this idea shortly, after we discuss an important distinction: As a rule, your novel will be inhabited by one main character and by everyone else.

Your Main Character

Even when an author employs the most distant third-person voice, writes a panoramic novel that is vision-driven rather than character-driven, or in some other way minimizes the importance of character, there is still usually one person in the novel with whom the author most identifies. In a panoramic novel like *War and Peace*, Tolstoy's three main characters, the innocent Natasha Rostov, the awkward Pierre Bezukhov, and the aristocratic Prince Andrew Bolkonsky, more serve the big ideas of the novel than fully come alive. Nevertheless, we feel that Tolstoy, who overtly identifies with

Pierre, has actually viscerally identified with Andrew, whose battlefield scene is the most intensely felt and realized moment in the novel. To this reader, Andrew is the main character of *War and Peace*.

As a rule, a novel will have only one such main character. Usually it is the heroine in a romance, the detective in a mystery novel, the "running man" in an adventure novel, the hero in a hero's journey novel, the poor idiot in a farce, the white-hatted cowboy in a Western. In a non-genre novel, it is the novel's protagonist: It is Raskolnikov in *Crime and Punishment* and Huck in *The Adventures of Huckleberry Finn*. Sometimes there is a division between a character who narrates and a main character whom the narrator observes and reports on, as, for instance, the division between Ishmael and Ahab in *Moby Dick*, Nick and Gatsby in *The Great Gatsby*, and Scout and Atticus in *To Kill a Mockingbird*. These real complications notwithstanding, as a rule there is one main character in every work of fiction: the character with whom the author wants us to concern ourselves the most.

It is interesting how little we need to know about the main character for us to feel drawn into the writer's story. We rarely know about the character's parents—or even that he had parents. We rarely know about where he went to school, where he traveled, what he read, whether he grew up in a city or in the woods, or even such everyday basics as his religion or his political affiliation. All a writer has to say is, "One day a nervous young man found himself wandering the streets of New York, contemplating murder," and we are off. Somehow, by that one sentence, we know almost all that we need to know. Isn't that remarkable?

That is all that *we* need to know. Does the writer need to know more? Does the writer need to sit down and create something like a biography for his character in order to know him or her well enough to proceed? Some writers may find that a valuable exercise, but the truest answer is a flat-out no. A writer can launch his novel without knowing much of anything about his character's background, and most writers, I would hazard to guess, operate exactly that way. A character comes to mind, maybe only as a fleeting image or a presence in the mind, and off the writer goes. He and his main character take off together and the story begins.

How is this possible? A committee that attempted to write a novel would assign three people the task of doing a background check on the character before launching the novel. A writer does something very different. She releases billions of neurons from their everyday tasks and commits them to forming what might be best thought of as a hologram of her character. That living, breathing person suddenly resides in her mind and is available to act on his own and interact with other characters. The character is really more alive than known to her, though he is known enough that if you brought the writer down to the station house and questioned her, she would be able to do a fine job of describing her character. It is just that she has no need to do that describing unless someone questions her. For her purposes, all she needs is the hologram. She wraps her arms around her character's neck, jumps on his back, and takes off headlong into the narrative.

This is beautiful and as it should be. A writer's best bet is to begin by allowing into existence the hologram of her main character. I've chosen the odd-sounding phrase "allow into existence the hologram of her main character" rather than the more conventional phrase "create her main character" because I want to underline the idea that characters more appear than are created. It is much more that a character enters the room than that we sit down at a drafting board. Something happens within us, we see something, feel something, or think something, and we turn to the computer to let that something out. The first line of our novel appears, or a scene arises, or two characters have an intense chat. Something waltzed into our brain and we moved that something as quickly as we could from our brain to a computer file.

A moment usually comes, however, when it pays a writer to think about her character in a more structured way. This may happen one minute into the writing or one month into the writing. It may come at a moment when the writer is suddenly unsure about her novel's plot or main idea. It may come on a dark day when she no longer likes the situation she dreamed up. It may come as a crisis moment, with the writer doubting that there is anything interesting or alive in her narrative, or a dull ache moment, with the writer resigned to continue but fearing the worst. Typically, we start out with enthusiasm and then grow unsure—sometimes about everything. When such a moment strikes, it may save the whole project to step back and do the work this book invites you to do: Learn more about your main character (and the other characters in your novel) and, by doing that, fall back in love with your book.

One Character, Two Characters, Three Characters, More

You may know your main character intimately—he or she may even be your alter ego. Typically, though, you know every other character in your novel less well, and sometimes so poorly that you have only the sketchiest idea of the makeup of the people surrounding your main character. The regularity with which this problem occurs may in fact be due to the way the brain operates. It may be the case that so many neurons are required for us to create a hologram of our main character—her voice, her attitude, her whole history and being—that we haven't enough neurons left to create holograms of the other characters. Or it may be that we get into the bad habit of supposing that we can get away with allowing our secondary characters to remain flat and unrealized.

At the same time, secondary characters sometimes seem more alive than main characters, usually because they have been drawn with a broad brush and possess the liveliness of simplicity and stereotype. The minor characters of Charles Dickens, for instance, are legendary for their liveliness and are often more memorable—and more interesting—than the Copperfield, Twist, or Nickleby for whom the novels is named. A secondary character can be a blowhard, a conniver, a great stoic, a comedienne, a good or bad witch, and because he or she is completely that thing, unburdened by the complexity of roundness, we experience that character as full of life. For these two reasons—that we are typically unaccustomed to delving deeply into our secondary characters and that we can get away with portraying them stereotypically—it becomes something of a habit that our secondary characters get short shrift.

This book provides you with the opportunity to get out of that habit. Instead of your villain playing one note, he can be invested with a whole range of actions and reactions, beliefs and opinions, foibles and even strengths. Instead of your love interest being just handsome and heroic, he can possess a real inner life, real fears and worries, real quirks and eccentricities, real dreams and aspirations. Instead of your main character's children squabbling stereotypically, they can squabble in richer ways rooted in their feelings about the particularly nasty divorce they endured or the particularly wrenching move they made from the suburbs to the inner city. As your understanding of each character deepens, your novel is enriched.

How many characters in your novel should you investigate and invigorate in this way? Does every doorman and every cab driver deserve or require this treatment? The short answer is: Investigate more characters rather than fewer ones. The process is so enjoyable and so rewarding that, if you can make the time and if you can get yourself in the habit, treat even quite minor characters as worthy of further investigation. Who knows: You may discover that the landlady you thought to describe in a sentence turns out to be crucial to the plot (as a confidante or a serial killer) or the second-banana buddy whom you thought to reserve for ridicule wants to emerge as a pillar of strength. When we give the characters in our novel the chance to become known to us, not only do we learn something about them but our characters start to grow right before our eyes.

Getting to Know Your Characters

Each novel comes into being differently from the next. In one you may have a complete sense of the plot and a whole cast of characters in mind from the outset. In another you may start with a main character and a hazy sense of the circumstances she will encounter and the characters she will meet. In a third you may start with exactly and only an idea, say the clash between two cultures, and no characters or plot. Because novels come into being in a different ways, sometimes completely populated and sometimes devoid of even a single character, it isn't possible to say, "Start using this book on day one so as to help yourself better understand your characters." On day one you may have no characters to understand.

A reasonable way to proceed is to start a cast of characters sheet for your current novel and, in the beginning, to operate with an understanding that characters may come and go before the cast is completely set. You may start your novel imagining that your main character is a young woman and learn, three days later, that she has to be a young man. Or she may stay a young woman—but now she hails from San Francisco, not Boise, and has grown from 5'2" to 5'8". You had her driving into town and stopping at a gas station, so a young mechanic had a place in the novel, but now you have her coming into town on a bus, so the young mechanic has been replaced by an African-American bus driver. You had her going to a fancy hotel that she couldn't afford, so you had a snooty desk clerk to draw, but now you have her staying at a residence for women run by nuns, so your snooty desk clerk has become a plump nun. During the early stages of writing a novel, changes of these sorts, and many more like them, are likely—if not bound—to occur.

Therefore your cast of characters list may end up looking like a baseball line-up card during an extra-inning game, with characters scratched out and new characters coming in to replace them. As a rule, however, a moment finally comes when your novel settles down and you know pretty well which players make up your cast of characters. Changes may still occur, new characters may appear as new plot points appear down the road, a given character may still morph, and even your main character may change slightly or dramatically. Nevertheless, once you settle into writing your novel and have acquired that settled feeling, such that your characters are beginning to interact even as you sleep, then you have arrived at a point where it may make sense to use this book.

I say *may* because I don't want to advocate over-analyzing your characters. If your characters feel rich and real to you and your novel is flowing, there is no reason to do anything but write your novel. There will be times, however, when it makes great sense to get to know a given character better. A character may pop into your mind and, as part of the process of judging whether he is a fit for your novel or interesting in his own right, you may decide to put him center stage and check him out. Or you may arrive at a stuck point in your novel, not know how to proceed, and reckon that visiting with your characters is exactly the right thing to do. For those times, this book can prove a real resource. Let me explain how to go about using it.

CHAPTER NO. 3

USING THIS BOOK

In this book, I'll present you with thirty situations into which you can drop your characters to discover how they might act and react. In reality, there are more than thirty situations available to you, because each situation comes with seven variations. The situations I present may be quite different from any that occur in the novel you're writing or intend to write, but they are designed to garner you important information about the workings of your characters' personalities.

The Program

Here are the twenty steps to follow if you want to make systematic use of these thirty scenarios.

1. Begin a Character Notebook

Whether you're jotting down character notes in a casual or a systematic way, you'll want a place to keep track of those notes. A notebook dedicated to your characters is a good idea. Set aside several pages in the notebook for each important character and a page or two for the minor characters. You'll want to dedicate several pages to the main characters because they may morph in important ways as you get to know them better.

One way to organize your notes is by employing the following twelve categories.

• **Basic headline.** Do you have a basic headline in mind that describes your character? For instance, when the creators of *All in the Family* were trying to decide on the character of Edith Bunker, it came to them that whatever Edith had to endure and whatever Archie Bunker might throw at her, she would react as Jesus Christ might have reacted. That headline allowed Jean Stapleton to know almost perfectly how she should play Edith in any situation. Such a headline isn't a necessity and you don't want to force a headline on your character, but if one emerges naturally it may prove of great value to you.

• **Basic history.** Every character has a basic history: an extended family of a certain sort, social, cultural, and religious roots, family myths and secrets (about issues like alcoholism, abuse, or depression), and family rules and customs. He or she also has the experience of pivotal childhood and adolescent events (like almost drowning, coming in first or last in a competition, etc.). There is almost certainly no need to know your character's history comprehensively. But you may want to get some of the basics down and add more as they become known to you through your investigations.

• **Archetypal, category, or stereotypical resonance.** You may enjoy considering whether and to what extent a given character partakes of some archetypal resonance. That is, does he or she resemble Aphrodite, Apollo, Zeus, or partake of what Victoria Schmidt in *45 Master Characters* calls "those largely unconscious image patterns that cross cultural boundaries"? Is your character fulfilling a category role, for instance, as the brusque police lieutenant who grudgingly helps your detective; the beautiful client who brings with her a whiff of sex, money, and danger; or the beautiful client's abusive-but-loving mob-connected husband? Is he or she living large as a needed stereotype (the best buddy, the Jewish mother-in-law, the imbibing priest)? If your character exists for reasons of this sort, you can make her richer and livelier by recognizing her archetypal, categorical, or stereotypical resonance and adding features and behaviors in line with (or, sometimes, against the grain of) that archetype, category, or stereotype.

• **Actions and reactions.** Each time you drop your character into one of the scenarios, you will learn a great deal about how your character acts and reacts. Your character is bound to activate different parts of her personality depending on whether she is flirting, taking part in a jury trial, being stalked, or engaged in a road adventure. Use your character notebook to record her various actions and reactions, making note of the particular circumstances that evoked the action or reaction. For example:

> I sense that Mary will be very sunny on her road adventure, singing along to CDs and stopping to chat with strangers, but on a jury she is going to be one of the quiet ones, careful to hide her thoughts and sometimes just nod-

ding her replies. In a way, both of these reactions are features of her serious nature—she is so light-hearted on her road adventure precisely *because* she is taking a conscious break from her serious side.

• **Moral valence.** Virtually every character in a novel has a moral valence: That is, the character comes across as more of a good person or more of a shady person. On balance, does your character seem trustworthy or untrustworthy, sober or impulsive, principled or unprincipled, kind or cruel? Is the protagonist's partner a good guy or on the take, is the protagonist's mother sweet and long-suffering or a ruthless bitch, is the protagonist's best friend solid as a rock or cynical and envious? If the idea makes sense to you that every character comes with a moral valence, then you will want to know at the very least whether to put a given character on the plus or the minus side of the ledger.

• **Dreams and ambitions.** Human beings have dreams and ambitions, even if they are ninety-year-old recluses or street people. A street person in New York may have the ambition to somehow make it to a warmer city, a ninety-year-old recluse may still dream of taking back the insult that was the last thing he said to his now-long-dead brother. Acquiring a sense of your character's dreams and ambitions is an excellent way to get to know your character's human side, a side that he may show only rarely but that is still an integral part of his personality.

• **Inner life.** Unless you've chosen a voice and a point of view that allow us into the heads of your characters, we can't know directly what your characters are thinking or what sort of inner life they are experiencing. But you can know directly by imagining how your character thinks, dreams, muses, fantasizes, and otherwise experiences her inner life. What is she thinking as she does the dishes (that's when Agatha Christie came up with her mystery plots)? What does she dream about? Is her inner talk negative and pessimistic or positive and optimistic? As you drop your character into each scenario, imagine what she is thinking as she chats with a distant cousin at a picnic, meets her new neighbors, or wakes from a vivid dream.

• **Shadow sides and difficulties in living.** Each of us has a shadow side; each of us experiences difficulties in living. Even your sweetest character has claws, no matter how well they may be retracted and hidden (hidden even from herself). Even your luckiest character has experienced pratfalls, blows to his self-image, and the occasional depression. For each character you investigate, stop for a minute and try to articulate his or her particular demons and his or her particular difficulties in living. Those difficulties might take the form of an incipient addiction, a propensity to ruin relationships, an inability to get over childhood issues, and so on.

- **Consequences of upbringing.** While no one can say for certain that a given behavior, attitude, or personality problem is the direct consequence of an individual's upbringing, you can decide to make that causal connection. You can decide in your own mind that your character's rage is directly related to the way his father always belittled him or that her chronic, disabling shyness is a direct result of her constantly being told by her mother that she should be seen and not heard. You can simplify causality and make these straight-line connections for the sake of fixing characters in your own mind and providing them with a singular source of motivation. As you investigate each of your characters, see if you want to set down any such causal connections.

- **Power, sexual potency, and alpha-ness.** Just as characters tend to come with a moral valence, they also tend to come with a power (and sexual power) valence, as someone who we perceive as powerful (and sexy) or weak (and not sexy). Even minor characters strike us as powerful or meek. This waiter seems powerful by virtue of the way he ignores his diners, that waiter seems meek by virtue of his obsequiousness. This secretary seems powerful because she saunters around the office, that secretary seems weak because she scurries around. If this idea makes sense to you, think through the power quotient (and sexiness quotient) of each character you choose to investigate.

- **Cultural component.** Every character is a representative of culture. He may be a minority member or a majority member of his culture, a conservative or a liberal, someone who goes exclusively to the symphony, exclusively to rock concerts, or to both, someone who buys his culture's values or is at war with those values. Culture creates stockbrokers and homegrown terrorists, Marines and anti-war activists, soccer moms and homeless families. Where does your character dine when she goes out (or does she just go out to eat)? What sport does she play? What does she watch on television? Such details help you understand the forces operating on your character and what piece she plays in the cultural puzzle.

- **Meaning web, beliefs, and opinions.** What is your character's meaning web?—that is, how do her beliefs and opinions knit together? What beliefs and opinions distinguish, for example, a conservative Republican from a liberal Democrat or a skeptical atheist from a fundamentalist believer? Beliefs and opinions of this sort are so real, deep-seated, firmly held, and internally consistent that you can predict with a high degree of certainty how a person who possesses this or that meaning web will react to any question or set of circumstances. If you can get a handle on it, how would you characterize the meaning web of the character you are investigating?

Use your character notebook to keep track in an organized way of the various bits of information that you gather about your character. In that way the information will remain available to you.

2. Begin a Second Notebook

In addition to your character notebook, you may want to start a second notebook in which you begin to keep other information about your current novel, for example, information about its plot (what happens), its setting (where it happens), and its ideas (why something happens). Indeed, you may discover that you are not only learning something about your characters by having them take a road adventure, participate on a jury, or attend a family picnic, but that a road adventure, jury trial, or family picnic actually has a place in your novel. As you drop your characters into the scenarios, have a second notebook handy so you can record whatever you learn that may prove useful.

3. Choose a Character

To begin with, work with one character at a time. (I'll discuss on page 26 how you can drop two or more characters into a scenario.) You might begin with your main character or with a character who is giving you trouble. Your starting place might be to make a master list of your characters (some of whom may vanish or morph as your novel progresses) and to keep that master list in your character notebook. If you have a master list of characters, study your master list and choose one character to investigate first.

4. Bring Your Character to Mind

Bring the character you've chosen to investigate fully to mind. Be patient and let him really enter your consciousness. Think a little about what you know about this character and what you don't know. In your character notebook, write down what you know already or what has just come to mind by inviting him to come forward. Ask your character to patiently wait as you proceed to the next step.

5. Choose a Situation

Look over the list of thirty situations. You can drop your character into all of them in turn or, if you are short of time or interest, you can choose just one or a few situations that seem most appropriate. If, for instance, you discover that you know nothing about your character's extended family, you might start with the family picnic scenario (page 28). If it strikes you that you are little uncertain about your character's sexual orientation, sexual prowess, or sexual interests, you might invite her into the sex shop (page 149). If there is a point in the novel where your character must step up to the plate and act heroically, you might begin with a moment of high drama (page 182) or sudden leadership (page 198). Decide which scenarios most serve your purposes with respect to this character and choose one scenario as your starting point.

6. Picture the Situation

Once you've chosen a character and a situation, get the situation in mind. If you've chosen the first scenario, a family picnic, picture the setting carefully. Then ask yourself, "Given this character, who will attend this picnic?" Fill the picnic with your character's relatives, getting as clear a picture as you can of her parents, siblings, in-laws, children, and so on. If you like, make a list of them and describe each family member in a little detail (overbearing older brother, feisty younger sister, etc.). Make this a specific, idiosyncratic picnic—this particular character's family picnic. Whichever scenario you choose, make sure that you can really picture it.

7. Address Each of the Six Questions

After you have a scenario clearly in mind, address in turn each of the six questions that I provide. For each of the questions:

• **Consider my responses.** For each question, I provide five possible responses. In fact, there are scores of responses possible and I have chosen five so as to give you a flavor of that range and to avoid making this an unwieldy book. As an exercise, you might try to compile a more comprehensive list of responses to the questions you encounter in this book, especially if you see yourself using the scenario with additional characters now and in the future.

• **Consider my interpretations.** A single behavior is not proof of character or personality. People with very different personality types might react exactly the same way in a given situation but for completely differ-ent reasons. A given behavior can, however, be suggestive of a particular personality and consistent with a given personality. That is what I have tried to provide in my interpretations, the sense of how a given behavior is consistent with a given personality type. To repeat: Just because a character *does* something doesn't mean that she *is* something. But that behavior is suggestive and will prove psychologically consistent much of the time.

• **Decide how your character might react.** Would your character have reacted in one of the five ways I describe, in a subtly different way, or in a radically different way? If you believe that your character would react in a way different from any of the responses I provide, get as clear a picture as you can of your character's response and then jot down some notes about what that response reveals about your character's personality, basic attitudes, and background.

• **Consider how your character might react early in the novel and later in the novel.** You may want to go a step further and ask yourself how your character might respond early in the novel and also later in the novel, especially if you are creating a character who changes or grows during the course of the novel. For instance, would he react the same way early in the novel and late in the novel to an invitation to visit privately with the president or to take on the role of jury foreperson? From this analysis you may not only discover how your character changes but also when and where in your novel these changes begin to appear.

• **Showcase your character's arc or growth.** You may also want to try to articulate your character's journey, for instance, from immaturity to maturity, from fearfulness to heroism, or from passivity to action. Once you've articu-lated that arc, locate points along that arc that represent significant changes for your character (these will usually take the form of pivotal events). Drop your character into the scenario right after each of these pivotal events to see how (and whether) he will react differently as he changes and grows.

8. Address My Additional Questions

In addition to the five questions I pose and discuss, I provide you with an additional question to reflect on. For example, in the family picnic sce-nario I ask you to think about what your character would do if she had to organize the picnic, if a fight erupted at the picnic between her mom and dad, or if a stranger crashed the picnic. Use any or all of these questions to further investigate your character's personality and reaction patterns.

9. Think Through the Additional Scenarios I Provide

In addition to inviting you to drop your character into the main scenario, I invite you to consider several alternative scenarios. For instance, in addition to or instead of employing the family picnic scenario, you might try your hand at a company picnic, a religious group picnic, or a high school reunion picnic. You might make it a habit of turning to the list of additional scenarios as a first step, in case it makes more sense to drop your character into one of the alternative scenarios rather than the main scenario. In any event, when you use one of the alternative scenarios, first get the scene clearly in mind and then create some useful situations (for instance, your character getting into a heated disagreement with his boss at a company picnic). Really experience your character in this alternative setting.

10. If You Like, Add Additional Questions and Scenarios

If you have the time, inclination, and need, you may find it useful to ask additional questions, create additional scenarios, and in other ways provide yourself with an enhanced learning experience. If you add questions and create alternative scenarios, you may want to make note of them so that you can use them with other characters and when you work on your future novels.

11. If You Still Don't Know What Your Character Would Do

If, after dropping your character into a given scenario and making use of the exercises provided, your character's nature still eludes you, address the following questions.

- Is this character eluding me because he doesn't really have a place in the novel?

- Is this character eluding me because I can't get past her archetypal or stereotypical nature (because she is pegged so one dimensionally)?

- Is this character eluding me because I don't really know what I want from this character or what role I expect him to serve in the novel?

- Is this character eluding me because I don't know enough about people of her sort (about medieval Italian dukes, geishas, poker professionals, heroin addicts, etc.)?

- Is this character eluding me because I'm asking him to do double duty, for instance, as a representative of a class or group and also as a love interest or villain?

- Is this character eluding me because she is so complex and/or changeable that I can't nail down her reaction patterns or personality?

- Is this character eluding me because he is so rigidly defined with respect to the main character, perhaps as the main character's foil?

- Is this character eluding me for some other reason that has suddenly occurred to me?

If these questions don't provoke a useful answer, your best bet is to proceed with the following steps, which, because they include dropping your character into new scenarios, are likely to provide you with the information you're seeking.

12. Consider the Follow-Up Discussion

After each scenario, I provide you with a brief discussion of some aspect of personality psychology that elaborates on ideas raised in the scenario. For example, I follow up the scenario elegant party (page 58), in which you'll be investigating your character's drinking habits (among other things), with a discussion of the warning signs of problem drinking and alcoholic drinking. These discussions may or may not relate directly to the character you're currently investigating but will deepen your understanding of personality issues.

13. Enjoy the "Did You Know?" Morsel

After each follow-up discussion, I'll provide you with a juicy tidbit related to the discussion. For instance, after the discussion of family dynamics and complexes that follows the family picnic scenario, I invite you to meet the original Electra, a pivotal character in the plays of Sophocles and Euripides and the namesake of Freud's Electra Complex.

14. Turn to Your Character Notebook

After the "Did you know?" tidbit, I provide you with three last "Food for Thought" questions. These questions are designed to spur further thought and to prime you to return to your character notebook. In addition to the "Food for Thought" questions, I end each section with some reminders about how to make use of your character notebook and your plot, setting, and idea notebook.

15. Put Your Character in Another Situation

Once you've completed a scenario, think through which, if any, of the other scenarios you want your character to visit. I recommend that you proceed through all thirty scenarios with each character, but if you haven't the time or inclination to proceed that systematically, at least consider making use of several scenarios.

16. Give Your Character a Vacation

After you've run your character through his or her paces in several scenarios and recorded your observations in your two notebooks, stop for a minute and consider your gut feeling about this character. Is he working? Are there important things you still need to know about his personality? Make a mental note or a literal note of your observations and then give the character a vacation.

17. Repeat the Process With a New Character

Once you've completed this process with one character, choose a new character and repeat the process. Return to your cast of characters and decide which character to investigate next.

18. Repeat the Process With a Pair of Characters

You may want to drop two characters in tandem into one or more of the scenarios. You might, for example, drop your main character and his love interest into the lovers' spat (page 239), caught in a big lie (page 214), or road adventure (page 141) scenarios. You might drop your main character and her foil or nemesis into the stalked (page 166), stranger in town (page 67), or moment of high drama (page 182) scenarios. People the scenarios with pairs of characters, so as to learn about their interpersonal dynamics.

19. Repeat the Process With Multiple Characters

If you're so inclined, you can repeat the process by dropping multiple characters into a given scenario to see how they might interact. Scenarios that are excellent for this purpose include jury duty (page 35), elegant party (page 58), family picnic (page 28), and sudden leadership (page 198).

20. If You Want to Learn More About Your Character

The best way to learn about your character is to spend real time with him, which systematically using this book encourages. Get to know your character's personality by allowing him or her to become your intimate, by taking notes, and—either sooner or later—by writing your character into existence!

THIRTY SCENARIOS
FOR YOUR CHARACTERS

SCENARIO NO. I

FAMILY PICNIC

Your character is attending an extended-family picnic. This may be the first time you meet any of your character's relatives, so give yourself adequate time to populate the picnic. Think through what sort of mother and father "made" your character, whether or not your character has siblings, and what the sibling order might be. Are there children, grandparents, important aunts and uncles, and/or important cousins, nephews and nieces? Take your time and begin to understand your character's extended family.

With your book in mind, dream up the right family picnic for your character to attend, one that will help you learn what you need to know. If you discover that your character's parents are deceased, will you place the picnic in the past or act as if they are still alive? Will you include the in-laws, if your character is married? Will you narrow the cast down to just your character's immediate family or will you include distant cousins? Take your time and develop your cast of characters and setting for your picnic.

1. What is the first thing your character does upon receiving an invitation to this extended family picnic?

A) Think about how she can get out of it?
B) Hope that a certain family member won't be there?
C) Look forward to seeing a certain family member?
D) Feel unaccountably depressed?
E) Call a family member to get the latest gossip?

A) Wanting to get out of the picnic is consistent with a character who is part of an extended family with real tensions present and who has decided that avoidance is the better part of valor.

B) Hoping that a certain family member isn't in attendance directs us to a specific dynamic between your character and another family member and sets the stage for an explosive or muted picnic conflict.

C) Looking forward to seeing a certain family member is consistent with a character who has the capacity to feel love and affection and who is likely in a successful long-term relationship.

D) Feeling unaccountably depressed alerts us to the possibility that your character sees herself as an outsider even in her own family.

E) Calling a family member to get the latest gossip brings to mind a chatty, enmeshed family where everybody knows—and is into—everybody else's business.

How does your character react upon receiving an invitation to an extended family picnic?

2. On the day of the picnic, does your character:

A) Dress carefully?
B) Dress eccentrically?
C) Wear comfortable clothes?
D) Dress sexily?
E) Dress shabbily?

A) Dressing carefully is consistent with a character who expects to be scrutinized and is feeling anxious and under pressure to perform.

B) Dressing eccentrically is consistent with a character who has developed into a free spirit and feels free of her family and their dynamics—or at least would like to believe that about herself.

C) Wearing comfortable clothes is consistent with a character who may really be free of family dynamics and doesn't perceive the picnic as a trial.

D) Dressing sexily is consistent with a character who is generally inappropriate, manifests addictive behaviors, and is likely on the grandiose, narcissistic—and depressed—side.

E) Dressing shabbily is consistent with a character who may be making a statement about her unworthiness or, alternatively, defiantly showing contempt and animosity for her family.

What will your character wear to the picnic?

3. How does your character greet her mother?

    A) With false love and enthusiasm?
    B) With genuine love and enthusiasm?
    C) Coolly?
    D) Carefully?
    E) Perfunctorily?

A) In many rule-bound families, it is the custom to put on a display of love and good cheer with the family matriarch, so such a display suggests a hidden nest of family rules and secrets.

B) Genuine love and enthusiasm are consistent with a strong, mentally healthy character who has received love in childhood.

C) Greeting her mother coolly suggests a significant level of hostility and unexpressed issues between mother and child.

D) Greeting her mother carefully is consistent with a defensive posture caused by receiving regular and repeated criticism and insults.

E) Greeting her mother perfunctorily is consistent with a distant relationship characterized by a lack of interest as much as a lack of love.

How does your character greet her mother?

∙∙∙∙∙∙∙∙∙∙∙∙∙∙∙∙∙∙∙∙∙∙∙∙∙∙∙∙∙ **⁇** ∙∙∙∙∙∙∙∙∙∙∙∙∙∙∙∙∙∙∙∙∙∙∙∙∙∙∙∙∙∙

4. How does your character greet her father?

   A) Gruffly?
   B) Coldly?
   c) Hotly?
   D) Defensively?
   E) Indifferently?

∙∙

A) A gruff greeting, especially between son and father but also between daughter and father, is consistent with a family dynamic of machismo, conventional gender roles, and working-class ethos.

B) A cold greeting suggests significant hostility and long-held grudges between child and parent.

c) A hot greeting, especially between daughter and father, suggests sexual dynamics and sexual secrets.

D) A defensive greeting suggests a history of criticism, rejection, bullying, and perhaps the severest forms of abuse.

E) An indifferent greeting suggests emotional distancing and a relationship that rises only to the level of civility.

How does your character greet her father?

∙∙∙∙∙∙∙∙∙∙∙∙∙∙∙∙∙∙∙∙∙∙∙∙∙∙∙∙∙ **⁇** ∙∙∙∙∙∙∙∙∙∙∙∙∙∙∙∙∙∙∙∙∙∙∙∙∙∙∙∙∙∙

5. How does your character spend her time at the picnic?

   A) Watching?
   B) Catching up?
   c) Getting high?
   D) Conversing with one other family member?
   E) Fulfilling a role?

∙∙

A) If your character watches, that is consistent with a character who has an intense inner life and who may be a rebel, thinker, and/or artist.

B) If she spends time catching up with family members, that is consistent with a character who possesses social graces and who knows how to act in social situations—irrespective of what she is actually feeling or thinking.

c) If your character gets high, that is consistent with a character who is uncomfortable in social situations and may also point to a substance abuse problem.

D) If your character spends most of her time with one other family member, that suggests that these two characters are confidantes, intimates, or like-minded.

E) If your character fulfills a role—as hostess, peacekeeper, troublemaker, etc.—that suggests she has trouble with autonomy and independent action.

How does your character spend her time at the picnic?

6. How would you describe the picnic?

    A) Cordial?
    B) Intense?
    c) Boring?
    D) Loving?
    E) Simmering?

A) A cordial picnic suggests the family at least knows how to look like it gets along, whether or not family members really love or like each other.

B) An intense picnic suggests high drama between at least two family members, perhaps a visiting son and his father or a pregnant daughter and her mother.

c) A boring picnic suggests a certain kind of family history from which your character may be escaping, for example, a history of conventionality, superficiality, and low aspirations.

D) A loving picnic suggests a warm, tolerant, good-humored extended family whose ups and down, difficulties, and disagreements do not prevent them from remaining close-knit.

E) A simmering picnic suggests enduring and shifting family conflicts and high drama in the lives of the family members.

How would you describe your picnic?

Situations to Consider

What would your character do if:

- She had to organize the family picnic?
- A fight erupted between her mom and dad?
- A stranger crashed the party?
- One of the younger guests vanished?
- A feuding family member arrived?
- A sibling invited her to join in a drinking game?
- She grew bored and wanted to leave?

Other Picnic Situations

Put your character in the most appropriate of the following situations and think through how she would act and react. If you like, flesh out the scene by adding one conflict and one surprise.

- a company picnic
- a picnic in the wilds, with danger lurking
- an intimate picnic on a lazy summer day by the lake
- a fancy, catered picnic with bluebloods
- a picnic into which your character accidentally wanders
- a religious group's Sunday picnic
- a high school reunion picnic

Family Dynamics

Families defy description. First of all, a family is always a snapshot in time: A family in 1995 is not the same collection of people as a family in 2005 or 2015. By 2015, the fifty-year-olds are now seventy, the five-year-olds are now twenty-five, and so on. Nor is the relationship between any two family members—mother and father, husband and wife, child and parent, sister and brother—static over time. For the sake of utility, you may want to get one powerful snapshot of your main character's extended family in mind, a snapshot of a moment in time that will help you remember the many family members and their interrelationships.

Psychological theory credits the parent-child relationship as the most important relationship in a person's life and the one with the most enduring influence on a person. Freud conjured with the ideas of an Oedipus

Complex (an intense, dynamic, and essentially unhealthy relationship between a son and his mother) and an Electra Complex (an intense, dynamic, and essentially unhealthy relationship between a daughter and her father). But we know from life and from literature that son-father and mother-daughter relationships can be just as dramatic as son-mother and daughter-father relationships. Whether your character is male or female, it is likely he or she has had and still has an intense relationship with both parents.

You may not be able to articulate in your own mind how family dynamics molded your character's personality, and you may suppose that family dynamics have no central or obvious place in your novel. For these two reasons, you may decide to skip thinking about your character's extended family and its influences on her. I suggest you don't skip this step. By bringing your character's extended family to mind—by inventing it, imagining it, and allowing it to live in your mind's eye—you will enrich your understanding of your character. You may also discover some family member or some family dynamic drops perfectly into your novel.

Did You Know?

The phrase *Electra Complex* comes from the plays of Euripides and Sophocles in which the character Electra drives her brother Orestes to kill their mother and her lover in revenge for the murder of their father. In simplest terms, the Electra Complex stands for the idea of a daughter's psychological and sexual obsession with her father.

Food for Thought

• Does your character have an ongoing relationship with her parents? If so, to what extent will that ongoing relationship factor into your novel?

• Does your character have a dynamic relationship with one or more siblings? Is there a place for that dynamism in your novel?

• Might the memory of a family member (like a grandparent or a parent) play a role in your novel?

SCENARIO NO. 2
JURY DUTY

Imagine that your character has been summoned for jury duty. First the summons arrives, then, perhaps a month or two later, your character must interrupt his life and go down to the courthouse to join a jury pool and wait to see if he will be impaneled on a jury. This scenario will help you investigate how your character reacts to authority, what his ideas are about civic duty, and what role he is likely to play in group situations.

As you investigate your character using this scenario, try to picture the courtroom and the trial's players as clearly as you can. Not only will this help you learn about your character, but it will also help you learn about courtroom scenes—scenes that appear regularly in genre and non-genre novels and that may have a place in a novel of yours one day. Change defendants, victims, defense attorneys, prosecutors, judges, locales (moving it, say, from Boston to the rural south to Vienna), and crimes. Try the scenario out as a criminal trial one time and a civil trial another. The trial-and-jury setting is an excellent one to learn well.

1. Your character receives a summons for jury duty. What is his first reaction?

A) Annoyance?
B) Cynicism?
C) Anxiety?
D) Excitement?
E) Indifference?

• •

A) Annoyance is consistent with a busy character who has a life that this jury summons has interrupted.

B) Cynicism is consistent with an educated character who is above average in intelligence, prone to bouts of depression, and anti-authority as a rule.

C) Anxiety suggests a character who fears the opinions of others, is frightened of authority, and may possess a perfectionistic streak that signals low self-esteem and inability to ever feel satisfied with his performance.

D) Excitement suggests a youthful, exuberant character and also a character who can easily put aside his current life for the sake of the novelty of a trial.

E) Indifference is consistent with a bored, jaded, and perhaps depressed character who has seen it all and who finds nothing thrilling—or who may be posing as someone bored and jaded, as an affectation.

What is your character's first reaction to receiving a jury summons?

• ⁉ •

2. Your character arrives for jury duty and waits for several hours in the convening room. During those hours does he:

A) Strike up a conversation with other potential jurors?
B) Pull out his laptop and answer e-mail?
C) Read a book?
D) Pace?
E) Plan his strategy for getting off the jury?

• •

A) Striking up a conversation with other potential jurors is consistent with a socialized, conventional character who is likely to espouse mainstream values or, alternatively, with a hungry character on the prowl for excitement or sex.

b) Pulling out his laptop and answering e-mail is consistent with a busy, professional character with many duties, responsibilities, goals, and aspirations.

c) Reading a book is consistent with a dreamy character with an active inner life and a penchant for fantasizing.

d) Pacing is consistent with a Type A character or with someone wound tight who, in a given set of circumstances, might explode.

e) Planning his exit strategy is consistent with a self-assured character who ranks personal pursuits over civic duty and who is not afraid to assert his individuality.

What does your character do as he waits to be impaneled?

3. Your character is called to a trial, learns that it is a rape trial, and must respond to a questionnaire to see if he would make a suitable juror. Does your character:

    A) Indicate a predisposition to doubt the prosecution?
    B) Indicate a predisposition to doubt the defense?
    C) Express strong feelings for the victims of crime?
    D) Express strong feelings for the rights of the accused?
    E) Claim to have no biases, prejudices, or opinions?

A) Indicating a predisposition to doubt the prosecution is consistent with a character who belongs to a minority culture, someone who has had run-ins with the law, or someone who is far to the right or far to the left (both of whom tend to doubt the motives of government).

B) Indicating a predisposition to doubt the defense is consistent with a law-and-order character with conventional, conservative values and stereotypical views of lawyers and criminals.

c) Although empathizing with the victim of a crime is a basic human reaction, expressing strong feelings for the victims of crime is consistent with a politically and psychologically conservative character.

D) Expressing strong feelings for the rights of the accused is consistent with an educated character who is politically and socially liberal.

E) Claiming to have no biases, prejudices, or opinions is consistent with a crafty character who hopes to get on this jury, or, more likely, a conventional, uneducated, defensive character with little insight into the realities of his own personality.

What does your character reveal on his jury questionnaire?

4. Your character is impaneled on the jury. Does he:

    A) Maintain a careful distance from the other jurors?
    B) Act friendly and conspiratorial?
    C) Act annoyed and put out?
    D) Not discuss the trial with anyone, as instructed?
    E) Discuss the trial with an intimate?

A) Maintaining a careful distance is consistent with a loner who has trouble relating to others.

B) Acting friendly and conspiratorial is consistent with a highly socialized character who is used to fitting into groups, joining cliques, and following rather than leading.

C) Acting annoyed and put out is consistent with a self-involved, perhaps grandiose or narcissistic character who is likely to dispute every group decision.

D) Not discussing the trial with anyone, as instructed, is consistent with a principled character or, more likely, an anal character who, to manage anxiety, is careful to abide by the rules—and to tattle on those who don't.

E) Discussing the trial with an intimate is consistent with a character who flouts rules or, equally likely, a character who likes to decide for himself what principles to uphold.

How does your character comport himself while on the jury?

5. Your character takes a dislike to someone else on the jury. Does your character:

    A) Ignore the other juror?

B) Occasionally bump into him?
c) Disguise his dislike and act friendly?
D) Confront the other juror?
E) Align with other jurors?

A) Ignoring the other juror is consistent with a self-contained character able to function well in the world.

B) Occasionally bumping into the other juror is consistent with a passive-aggressive character or, alternatively, with a character with a good bit of whimsy and the trickster in him.

c) Disguising his dislike and acting friendly is consistent with a manipulative character who is likely ambitious and untrustworthy.

D) Confronting the other juror is consistent with an oppositional, angry, and impulsive character who may incline toward violence.

E) Aligning with other jurors is consistent with a weak-willed character who finds strength in numbers or a controlling character who knows how to use others to serve his own needs and ends.

What would your character do if he took a dislike to another juror?

6. The jury is deliberating and the vote is 10 to 2 in one direction or the other. Your character is one of the two holdouts. What will he do?

A) Ask to hear certain evidence or arguments repeated?
B) Look for ways to join the majority?
c) Argue with other jurors?
D) Staunchly defend his position?
E) Silently stick to his guns?

A) Asking to hear certain evidence or arguments repeated is consistent with a character who favors reason and rationality and who likes to have his position buttressed by logic and facts.

B) Looking for ways to join the majority is consistent with a social-ized character who is independent enough to have a nonconforming opinion but not independent enough to stick with that opinion in the face of opposition.

c) Arguing with the other jurors is consistent with an oppositional character who may be most interested in staking out a contrary position.

d) Staunchly defending his position is consistent with a highly principled character or a highly obstinate character—or someone who is both.

e) Silently sticking to his guns is consistent with a victimized member of a minority with a stoic personality.

What would your character do if his was the minority opinion?

Situations to Consider

What would your character do if:

- The case involved a freedom of speech issue?
- The case involved a reproductive rights issue?
- Your character found the defendant sexually attractive?
- Your character heard jurors make up their mind right at the outset?
- The judge admonished your character for not paying attention?
- Your character was offered a bribe to vote a particular way?
- The case involved the death penalty?

Other Group Situations

Put your character in the most appropriate of the following situations and think through how he would act and react. If you like, flesh out the scene by adding one conflict and one surprise.

- in a lifeboat
- on a company softball team
- stuck in a crowded elevator
- on a walking tour of England
- in a board meeting
- in a tug-of-war at a picnic
- as a member of a platoon in combat

Be Your Own Jury Consultant

A good way to better understand the characters in your novel is to think like a jury consultant. In a given case, with a particular plaintiff, a particular defendant, and a particular charge, who would you want on your jury if you were an attorney for the plaintiff, and who would you want on your jury if you were an attorney for the defendant?

Trial consultant Howard Varinsky explained in "Directing Voir Dire," an article that appeared in the legal journal *The Recorder*:

> In criminal cases, prosecutors like traditional law-and-order, conservative types, while defense attorneys look for minorities and liberals. This is because minorities are thought to distrust police and be cynical about the criminal justice system, and liberals tend to empathize with the underdog and champion the rights of defendants. These stereotypes work much of the time. However, in some cases they don't. The William Kennedy Smith date rape case provides an excellent counter-example. The jurors were all older, educated, religious, conservative and traditional. Normally, this type of jury is a prosecutor's dream. In a date rape case, however, the victim is also on trial and in this case it would have been difficult to get an acquittal with the stereotypical criminal defense jury.

Think like a trial consultant. Like writers, they are among our real psychologists. Regularly use the jury duty scenario, sometimes placing your character on the jury and sometimes making him the defendant.

Did You Know?

Does a prospective juror answer questions more truthfully during the *voir dire* process, with the judge and his peers watching, or on the jury questionnaire he fills out before the trial begins? By far, on the pre-trial questionnaire! Varinsky explained:

> Peer pressure, the perception of the judge as an authority figure, and the instinctive need to be accepted make prospective jurors less candid when sharing their personal views in open court than when answering questions privately.

Food for Thought

• What aspect of the jury system is most aligned with your character's personality and values?

• What aspect of the jury system is least aligned with your character's personality and values?

• Given your character's history and personality, if he were part of the court system, would he more likely be a defense attorney, prosecutor, judge, defendant, bailiff, court reporter, or clerk of the court?

SCENARIO NO. 3
POOLSIDE ENCOUNTER

Imagine that your character is on vacation in some tropical paradise. Instead of going to the beach this morning, as the sea is still a little chilly, she goes down to the pool to read and soak up some early morning rays. Although the pool area is empty, when a stranger enters the pool area he pulls up a chaise very near your character and after a while engages your character in conversation. Not long after sitting down, the stranger asks your character a very personal question.

Decide in your own mind what sort of personal question the stranger asks. It might be a personal question about your character's race or ethnicity (e.g., "You sort of look Jewish to me—are you Jewish?"). It might be a personal question about her finances (e.g., "I've never been able to save—have you saved a lot?"). It might be a personal question about her sex life (e.g., "You look like you do all right with the fellows—are you pretty successful?"). Get your character in mind, pick an appropriate stranger with an appropriately inappropriate question, and consider the following questions.

· ·

1. Does your character respond only if:

   A) She finds the stranger attractive?

B) She finds the stranger safe?

C) She finds the stranger interesting?

D) She finds the stranger dangerous?

E) She finds the stranger familiar?

· ·

A) Responding because she finds the stranger attractive is consistent with a sexually abused or exploited character who has poor boundaries, or, alternatively, with someone looking for a harmless flirtation who is willing to divulge so as to keep the conversation going.

B) Responding because she finds the stranger safe is consistent with a naïve character who inclines toward gullibility and who trusts too easily.

C) Responding because she finds the stranger interesting is consistent with a bored character in need of excitement or, alternatively, with an intellectual character intrigued by the nature of the interaction.

D) Responding because she finds the stranger dangerous is consistent with a weak-willed character who is easily bullied into revealing too much or, alternatively, with a thrill-seeking character looking for danger.

E) Responding because she finds the stranger familiar is consistent with a socialized character who categorizes people according to whether they belong to her group, clique, or social class.

Under what circumstances would your character reply?

· ·

2. If your character chooses to reply, how does she reply?

A) Evasively?

B) With embarrassment?

C) With annoyance?

D) Intimately?

E) Matter-of-factly?

· ·

A) An evasive reply is consistent with a sly character who is likely to be evasive in other aspects of her life as well, for instance, in relationships or at work.

B) Replying with embarrassment is consistent with an anxious and perhaps easily manipulated character who worries about what other people think.

c) Replying with annoyance is consistent with a short-tempered, perhaps impulsive character who acts out in social situations.

D) Replying intimately is consistent with a character who regularly discloses too easily, perhaps because of early sexual abuse or as a result of growing up with alcoholic parents.

E) Replying matter-of-factly is consistent with a self-confident character who is easy with self-disclosure, doesn't feel threatened by people, and believes she has the situation under control.

How would your character reply?

3. If your character replies and the stranger asks another intimate question, what would your character do?

    A) Answer?
    B) Tell the stranger off?
    c) Turn away in embarrassment?
    D) Turn away in anger?
    E) Leave?

A) Answering a second time suggests either some weakness of character or some real interest in the stranger—or both.

B) Telling off the stranger is consistent with a character who can put up with a degree of rudeness in others and is willing to answer one personal question, but who also possesses sensible boundaries and sees two questions as one too many.

c) Turning away in embarrassment is consistent with a character who is easily intimidated by others and perhaps also easily manipulated.

D) Turning away in anger is consistent with a character who is unwilling to be pushed around and refuses to be made to leave, but who is also likely to let pressures and complaints build up inside.

E) Getting up and leaving is consistent with a self-confident character who understands that not making a fuss is the surest way to end an unpleasant interaction of this sort.

What would your character do if she were asked a second personal question?

• **⁇** •

4. Imagine that in response to the stranger's question your character lies. Why has she lied?

   A) To protect her privacy?
   B) Out of fear?
   C) Out of embarrassment?
   D) To get one over on the stranger?
   E) To teach the stranger a lesson?

A) Lying to protect her privacy is consistent with a character who is self-protective, secretive, and perhaps a bit of a recluse.

B) Lying out of fear is consistent with a character who has experienced emotional or corporal punishment and who perhaps uses lying as a primary defense mechanism.

C) Lying out of embarrassment is consistent with a shy, mild-mannered, anxious personality who is easily flustered and put off her game.

D) Lying to get one over on the stranger is consistent with a competitive, combative personality, someone likely to drive a hard bargain and be successful in business.

E) Lying to teach the stranger a lesson is consistent with a vengeful character or, alternatively, with a trickster character with a wry personality.

Why would your character lie?

• **⁇** •

5. If your character refuses to reply and the stranger insists, what will your character do?

   A) Turn away from the stranger?
   B) Tell the stranger off?

c) Give in and reveal the information?

d) Get up and leave, but courteously?

e) Get up and leave, but angrily?

• •

A) Turning away is consistent with a self-composed character who possesses a solid self-image and the ability to act calmly and quietly on her core convictions.

B) Telling the stranger off is consistent with an impulsive character who lacks the ability to hold her own counsel and who likely has ruined relationships and business opportunities through intemperate outbursts.

c) Giving in and revealing the information is consistent with a weak, anxious character with a history of failures and disappointments who is primed to buckle under pressure.

D) Getting up and leaving in a courteous way is consistent with a character with good social skills who functions well in the world and is adept at handling even the most difficult interpersonal situations.

E) Getting up and leaving angrily is consistent with a passionate, intense character who takes pride in always openly expressing her emotions, even the negative ones.

If the stranger persists, what will your character do?

• •

6. If your character reveals the information, what will her reaction be later?

A) Annoyance at having revealed so much?

B) Anger at having revealed so much?

c) Amusement at having revealed so much?

D) Guilt at having revealed so much?

E) Indifference?

• •

A) Annoyance at having revealed so much is consistent with a character who experiences some guilt in life but who is able to put matters in perspective and ultimately forgive herself.

B) Anger at having revealed so much is consistent with a character at war with the world or, alternatively, with someone who tends to be very hard on herself.

C) Amusement at having revealed so much is consistent with an ironic character at ease with herself who tends to be philosophical and phlegmatic by nature.

D) Guilt at having revealed too much is consistent with an anxious character burdened by strict, inflexible ideas about what constitutes right and wrong behavior.

E) Indifference at having revealed too much is consistent with a bored character who doesn't get worked up about anything, or, alternatively, with a thick-skinned character who lets external and internal criticism roll off her back.

If your character reveals personal information to a stranger, what will her reaction be later?

Situations to Consider

What would your character do if:

- The stranger turned out to be a private detective?
- The stranger turned out to be a scam artist?
- Your character revealed far too much?
- Your character suddenly recognized the stranger?
- Someone known to the stranger joined them?
- Someone known to your character joined them?
- The stranger gave a startling reason for asking?

Other Information Situations

Put your character in the most appropriate of the following situations and think through how she would act and react. If you like, flesh out the scene by adding one conflict and one surprise.

- being tested for a sexually transmitted disease
- first visit to a therapist
- consultation with a financial advisor
- religious confession
- in bed with a lover
- interrogated as a prisoner of war
- interviewed on television

47

Appropriate Self-Disclosure

It is one thing to be able to disclose important information about yourself, including very private information. That ability is a sign of strength and mental health. It is another thing to actually make those disclosures: Disclosing depends on the circumstances. A person with the ability to disclose might do so readily and often in an intimate relationship but, for common-sense reasons, never do so with a poolside stranger.

Conversely, a person who has great trouble disclosing may make inappropriate disclosures to virtual strangers, especially after a few drinks, exactly because she is so used to rigidly withholding. Because so much pressure has built up inside, that pressure occasionally causes an explosion of inappropriate self-disclosure.

Clinical psychologist Clayton Tucker-Ladd explained in *Psychological Self-Help*:

> How do you know what is appropriate disclosure? First of all, you should have a reason to disclose. Second, you should consider (1) how much you have already disclosed, (2) who you are talking to—your best friend? a new acquaintance? a parent? a boss? a mutual helping group?—and (3) how much can the disclosure hurt you? When these three factors are considered, most of us have a feel for what is appropriate.

Get in the habit of putting your characters in practice situations where self-disclosure is appropriate and where self-disclosure in inappropriate. Think through how they might disclose or withhold various kinds of information: about a black sheep sibling, a financial mishap, a sexual problem, a strain of insanity in the family, a moment of keen embarrassment. Learn whether your character *can* self-disclose; and in which circumstances she *would* self-disclose.

Did You Know?

As a rule, people don't like it if men disclose too much or women disclose too little. Tucker-Ladd explained:

> Women can disclose more to strangers or new acquaintances than men can and still be liked. For example, a women is, in general, liked if she reveals that her mother or father recently committed suicide or that she has certain sexual preferences (not homosexuality, though). A man is not liked if he

discloses the same information. However, neither women nor men are liked if they share nothing about themselves.

Food for Thought

• When would your character reveal very personal information, and when wouldn't your character reveal such information?

• About what would your character be most close-lipped: ethnic/racial information, financial information, or sexual information?

• Under what circumstances would your character ask another person a very personal question?

SCENARIO NO. 4

FENDER-BENDER

Your character is out driving. Carefully set the scene in your mind, picturing the make and model of your character's car, its luxuriousness or ordinariness, the neighborhoods through which your character drives, the music playing on the CD player, the mood your character is in. Where is he going? How much traffic is around? What is the weather like? Set the scene carefully both for the sake of this exercise and because you're likely to employ many driving scenes in the novels that you write.

While driving, your character is involved in a minor accident. An accident is a good test of a character's personality, because people tend to react as they really are in the split second after an accident occurs. Within seconds their social mask is likely to return, but for an instant, you can catch a glimpse of their true personality. Ride with your character and be observant, especially at the moment of impact.

1. Imagine that the fender-bender is your character's fault. How will he react?

   A) Defensively?
   B) Apologetically?

c) Angrily?

d) Anxiously?

e) Indifferently?

. . . .

A) A defensive reaction is consistent with a character who is self-protective, prepared to lie, and indifferent to taking personal responsibility for his actions.

B) An apologetic reaction is consistent with a warm, open, honest character or, alternatively, with a character schooled in social graces and the importance of appearances.

C) An angry reaction, when the accident is his fault, is consistent with an arrogant, narcissistic, and likely violent personality.

D) An anxious reaction is consistent with a character who is likely to manifest significant anxiety in other aspects of his life, including his work life, creative life, and sex life.

E) Reacting indifferently is consistent with a down-and-out character who is used to getting the short end of the stick, with someone too tired and depressed to react, or with a very cool customer.

How does your character react if the accident is his fault?

. . . .  . . . .

2. Imagine the fender-bender is the other person's fault. How will your character react?

A) Compassionately?

B) Angrily?

C) Suspiciously?

D) Matter-of-factly?

E) Unconcernedly?

. . . .

A) A compassionate reaction is consistent with a character who is principled, able to empathize, and likely in an enduring long-term relationship.

B) An angry reaction is consistent with a character who is hot-headed, quick to judge, unwilling or unable to empathize, and likely burdened by addiction issues.

c) A suspicious reaction is consistent with a reclusive, skeptical, and perhaps paranoid character who displays mistrust in most of his daily affairs.

D) A matter-of-fact reaction is consistent with a mature character with a certain amount of life experience who is philosophical and phlegmatic by nature.

E) Showing too little concern is consistent with a highly anxious character who is dissociating himself from the moment or, alternatively, with a reckless character who experiences an adrenaline rush, rather than worry, at the scene of an accident.

How does your character react if the accident is the other person's fault?

3. What would your character's first reaction to the accident be?

    A) Relief not to be injured?
    B) Annoyance about the insurance repercussions?
    c) Worry for the other driver's condition?
    D) Irritation at being inconvenienced?
    E) Fear about the other driver's reaction?

A) If your character's first reaction is relief at not being injured, that may suggest a recent history of mishaps and accidents or a particular trauma from which your character still hasn't recovered.

B) If your character's first reaction is annoyance about the insurance repercussions, that suggests your character may have his feet firmly planted in the real world of duties and responsibilities and can't tolerate the thought of dealing with yet another red-tape task.

c) If your character's first thought is about the other driver's condition, that may suggest either a compassionate nature or a worry that this minor accident may escalate into something more complicated if the other driver is injured.

D) If your character's first reaction is irritation, that suggests a self-absorbed character busily on the run who dislikes having his agenda interrupted.

E) If your character's first reaction is one of fear about the other driver's reaction, that may suggest a character used to abusive situations where minor incidents and irritations lead to violence.

What is your character's first reaction to the accident?

4. Your character's car is slightly damaged. How does he react to that damage?

    A) Philosophically?
    B) Angrily?
    C) Anxiously?
    D) Indifferently?
    E) So strongly as to want a new car?

A) If your character takes a little damage philosophically, that is consistent with someone who is not overly attached to material possessions and who probably views the very ideas of consumerism and materialism with some skepticism and distaste.

B) If he reacts angrily, that is consistent with a character who values possessions highly and maybe even prizes them above people.

C) If your character reacts anxiously, that is consistent with a character who has had the value of material objects instilled in him, perhaps as a result of corporal punishment.

D) If he reacts indifferently, that is consistent with a character who is alienated from the culture and who makes a point of disputing his culture's values.

E) If he reacts so strongly that a new car is wanted, that is consistent with a fragile character susceptible to splitting—to finding things (and people) either all good or all bad. Undamaged, the car was perfect; with a dent in it, the car is now suddenly ruined and worthless.

How would your character react to some damage?

5. What is the first thing your character does upon getting home?

    A) Pour himself a drink?
    B) Call someone to talk about the accident?
    C) Take a nap?

D) Kick the cat?

E) Go about his business?

. . . .

A) Pouring a drink is consistent with a character who is in the habit of using substances to gain relief from anxiety, especially if it's still morning when he returns home and starts drinking.

B) Calling someone to talk about the accident is consistent with an extraverted, socialized character whose custom is to share news with and get help from friends and family.

C) Taking a nap is consistent with a fragile, anxious, and perhaps depressed character who can be laid low, at least for a while, by small incidents and accidents.

D) Kicking the cat is a classic displacement reaction, where a person expresses anger at an inappropriate object, and is consistent with a character with poor impulse control and a lack of empathy.

E) Going about his business is consistent with a stoic character who lets things build up inside but refuses to show discomfort or, alternatively, with a well-adjusted character who in fact is taking this fender-bender in stride.

What is the first thing your character does upon getting home?

6. What is most true about your character the next day?

  A) The accident is still on his mind a lot?
  B) The accident is still on his mind, but only a little?
  C) He isn't thinking about the accident but feels quite shaky?
  D) He isn't thinking about the accident but feels a little shaky?
  E) Your character has completely forgotten about the fender-bender?

. . . .

A) If the accident is still on his mind a lot the next day, that is consistent with a character who has trouble letting go of negative events and is probably burdened by a memory bank full of traumatic incidents.

B) If the accident is still on his mind a little, that is consistent with a character who processes events to see if there is anything that needs to be done (like double-check with his insurance agent) but who isn't overburdened by events in the past.

C) If he isn't consciously thinking about the accident but is feeling quite shaky, that is consistent with an anxious, fragile character who may not be very good at identifying the sources of his anxiety.

D) If he isn't consciously thinking about the accident but is still feeling a little shaky, that is consistent with a character with sufficient strengths to successfully negotiate life but with a range of emotional vulnerabilities as well.

E) If your character has completely forgotten about the accident, that is consistent with a character with little conscience and impulse control who is likely to keep getting into trouble or, alternatively, with a mentally healthy character who is able to exorcise the sting of minor negative events almost as quickly as they occur.

What is your character thinking and feeling the next day?

Situations to Consider

What would your character do if:

- The fender-bender occurred in a foreign country?
- The fender-bender occurred in a high crime area?
- The other driver was pregnant?
- The other driver looked dangerous?
- The other driver was sexually attractive?
- The other driver was obviously drunk?
- Your character had important business elsewhere?

Other Accidental Situations

Put your character in the most appropriate of the following situations and think through how he would act and react. If you like, flesh out the scene by adding one conflict and one surprise.

- your character cuts a finger, and it bleeds profusely
- your character trips and falls on the sidewalk
- your character is just barely nudged by a car as he's crossing in a pedestrian crosswalk

- your character's back goes out while he is on vacation
- your character drops an expensive antique
- your character injures himself playing sports
- your character suffers a mild case of food poisoning

Auto Accidents and Post-Traumatic Stress

When a character experiences a trauma, you can predict a reasonable likelihood that the effects of the trauma will linger. Some typical effects are avoiding conversations about the event; avoiding activities, people, and places that might arouse recollections of the event; difficulties falling or staying asleep; irritability and outbursts of anger; and so on. When a number of these effects are present, post-traumatic stress disorder is the clinical diagnosis. You can use any of these effects (or symptoms) to paint a picture of a character who has undergone trauma.

Researchers Dennis Butler, Steven Moffic, and Nick Turkal explained in "Post-Traumatic Stress Reactions Following Motor Vehicle Accidents" published in *American Family Physician* magazine:

> Most Americans will be involved in a motor vehicle accident in their lifetime, and one quarter of the population will be involved in accidents that result in serious injuries. Vehicular accidents sometimes lead to post-traumatic stress symptoms. Traffic accidents have become the leading cause of post-traumatic stress disorder (PTSD) since the Vietnam War. It is estimated that 9 percent of survivors of serious accidents develop significant post-traumatic stress symptoms and that many other survivors have PTSD-like reactions.

When you drop a character into the fender-bender scenario, think through if this minor accident will have any lasting effects. If you sense that it might, what does that tell you about your character's personality? Is he more fragile, anxious, or sensitive than you first supposed?

Did You Know?

Can your character develop PTSD even after an accident as minor as a fender-bender? Absolutely! An important clue is the presence of nightmares immediately after the accident. Butler, Moffic, and Turkal explain:

> Horrific and intrusive memories immediately following a motor vehicle accident are a strong predictor of PTSD symptoms, regardless of the severity of the accident or the injuries.

Food for Thought

• People tend either to internally slow down or to speed up when an accident occurs. Is your character more likely to internally slow down or speed up?

• Is your character accident-prone? What are the personality traits of someone who is accident-prone?

• Is your character someone who tends to shoulder responsibility or blame others? In the context of a fender-bender, what would shouldering responsibility or blaming others look like?

SCENARIO NO. 5
ELEGANT PARTY

Your character has been invited to attend an elegant party at the home of people important to the life of your prospective book. Maybe these people are the parents of your heroine's love interest, the couple that hold the clue to solving the mystery that your sleuth is investigating, or people who represent the social class your character would love to enter or is eager to escape.

With your book in mind, dream up the right elegant party for your character to attend, one in keeping with the logic, meaning, and plot of your novel. Spend a few minutes writing out a brief description of the party—what the home looks like, what occasion is being honored, what sorts of people are attending—so as to help anchor the scene in your mind. Then answer the following questions.

1. What is the first thing your character does upon receiving this invitation?

 A) Smile ironically?
 B) Have a double Scotch—and then another?
 C) Excitedly call a friend?
 D) Think about what she will wear?
 E) Plan to refuse?

A) An ironic smile speaks volumes about what your character thinks about social class and social interactions like parties and is consistent with a character with deeply held beliefs about fairness and justice.

B) Having a few drinks might alert us to a serious problem she is having with managing stress and is consistent with a character with addictive tendencies who likely also smokes and goes on sugar binges.

C) Excitedly calling a friend gives us the sense that your character is more extroverted than introverted and may rely too heavily on the opinions of others and is consistent with a jovial, conventional character.

D) Thinking about what clothes she might wear alerts us to the possibility that your character is overly concerned about appearances and is consistent with a character constrained by social roles and rules.

E) Planning to refuse is consistent with a self-assured character who is able to turn down even A-list invitations or, alternatively, with a narcissistic, self-sabotaging character who refuses out of grandiosity.

What is the first thing your character does upon receiving this invitation?

2. The day of the party arrives. How does your character react in the hours leading up to the party? Is she:

    A) Ironic and indifferent?
    B) Excited and eager?
    C) Worried and anxious?
    D) Dangerous and sinister?
    E) Cool and calculating?

A) An ironic, indifferent reaction is consistent with a character who prefers her own company, sees social events as empty and meaningless necessary evils, and will likely be the first one to leave the party.

B) An eager, excited reaction is consistent with a youthful, exuberant, and naïve character who is likely looking for love and adulation and who sees social gatherings of this sort as opportunities to shine.

c) A worried, anxious reaction is consistent with a character with few social graces and a phobia about social interactions who is likely worried about what to wear, how to act, and what to say.

d) Acting in a sinister manner is consistent with an antisocial, perhaps criminal character who sees a gathering of wealthy guests as a chance to run a scam or engage in even darker mischief.

e) Acting cool and calculating is consistent with a character who prides herself on her ability to negotiate social situations to her advantage and who is thinking through what she might personally gain from this evening's festivities.

How would you portray your character in the hours leading up to the party?

3. Your character arrives at the party. The hostess greets her snidely and high-handedly. What does your character do?

    A) Respond indignantly?
    B) Smile, say nothing, and begin drinking heavily?
    C) Recoil and think about leaving?
    D) Obsess about what she did to provoke such a greeting?
    E) Calmly ask the hostess for an explanation?

A) Responding indignantly is consistent with a proud character who isn't intimidated by grand hostesses and who prides herself on speaking her mind and refusing to take guff from anyone.

B) Smiling, saying nothing, and drinking heavily is consistent with an ironic, perhaps intellectual and artistic character who sees herself as above reacting to insults but who doesn't realize that her forced silence comes with a price, one that she pays by drinking.

C) Recoiling and thinking about leaving is consistent with a nervous, thin-skinned character who has trouble defending herself and has probably been steamrolled many times in the past, by family and strangers alike.

D) Obsessing about what she did to provoke such a greeting is consistent with a highly anxious, brooding character with low self-esteem who is quicker to blame herself than to blame others.

E) Calmly asking the hostess for an explanation is consistent with a naïve, child-like character like a Forrest Gump or, alternatively, with a highly evolved person like a Gandhi or a Martin Luther King, Jr.

How would your character react if she were insulted by the party's hostess?

4. The party is in its second hour. Your character has spent several minutes eyeing someone attractive. Finally, that person glances over, makes eye contact, and smiles. What does your character do?

    A) Blush and look away?
    B) Hold eye contact for a long instant and then look away?
    C) Hold eye contact until the other person looks away?
    D) Come directly over?
    E) Smile and hoist her drink by way of greeting?

A) Blushing and looking away is consistent with a shy, youthful, easily embarrassed character who is likely generally self-conscious and awkward in social situations.

B) Holding eye contact for a long instant and then looking away is consistent with a sly character who enjoys romance and intrigue, and relishes posing as a mysterious stranger in social situations.

C) Holding eye contact until the other person looks away is consistent with a fiercely controlling and possibly violent character who takes pride in never giving in.

D) Coming directly over is consistent with a bold, brash character who goes after what she wants and is likely opinionated, outspoken, and nobody's fool.

E) Smiling and hoisting her drink by way of greeting is consistent with a sociable character who enjoys making contact with strangers but who also feels it wise to maintain boundaries and not leap right in.

What would your character do if she made eye contact with an attractive stranger?

5. Several guests are intimately chatting in a small sitting room. It is important that your character make contact with one of the people in that room. Does your character:

A) Locate a bowl of nuts or a cheese tray and use it as an excuse to make an entrance?

B) Stride in, say "Hello!" and directly ask the person for a word?

C) Sidle in, hang around uncomfortably, and wait for the right moment to speak?

D) Ask someone else to go in and give the person a message?

E) Skip trying, even though there will be negative consequences to not making contact?

A) Locating a bowl of nuts and using it as an excuse is consistent with a savvy character with a playful streak who likely pulls pranks and is amused by the fact that social interacting requires so much game-playing.

B) Striding in and directly asking for a word is consistent with a bold, powerful character who takes pride in standing up in life or, alternatively, with a scared character who manages to deal with her fear by posing as someone bold.

c) Sidling in and hanging around uncomfortably is consistent with an anxious character with few social graces and a diminished sense of self-esteem who sees her rightful place as far in the background.

D) Asking someone else to go in is consistent with a weak-willed, frightened character who has trouble with autonomous action and with expressing her needs.

E) Not trying, even though there will be negative consequences, is consistent with a pessimistic, defeated character who is likely depressed, both by all that hasn't gone her way already and by new defeats on the horizon, like this one.

What would your character do if she needed to communicate with someone engaged in intimate group conversation?

6. Your character has gotten a little tipsy. Would your character:

A) Drive home but drive slowly and cautiously?

B) Drive home without making allowances for her state of intoxication?

c) Stop drinking for two hours before driving home?

D) Ask the hostess to call a cab?

E) Ask the hostess if she can spend the night?

A) Driving home but driving slowly and cautiously is consistent with a conventional, socialized character who doesn't mind breaking the law as long as she isn't breaking it too much.

B) Driving home without making allowances for her state of intoxication is consistent with an impulsive character who likely crashes regularly—literally, in her car, and metaphorically, in life.

c) Not drinking for two hours before driving home is consistent with a character who is prudent enough to take some precautions but not so prudent as to forego driving entirely, analogizing to a life marked by general steadiness and occasional crises.

D) Asking the hostess to call a cab is consistent with a cautious character who may be guided as much by her desire to look responsible and above reproach as by her inclination to do the right thing.

E) Asking the hostess if she can spend the night is consistent with a strong-willed character who has the gumption to ask for what she believes she needs, even if what she needs is a guest bedroom in a relative stranger's home.

What would your character do if she had gotten tipsy at a party and faced the question of driving home under the influence?

Situations to Consider

What would your character do if:

• The party was canceled?
• A fight broke out at the party?
• She were cornered by an obnoxious guest?

• A guest stopped breathing?
• An argument broke out along racial lines?
• She felt sexually aroused?
• An old nemesis appeared?

Other Party Situations

Put your character in the most appropriate of the following situations and think through how she would react. Flesh out the scene by adding one conflict or one surprise.

• a suburban pool party
• a large ethnic wedding
• a reception following a gay marriage
• a church-sponsored potluck picnic
• a pub get-together for singles
• an intimate dinner for three couples
• an after-hours party an alternative music club

Party Drinking

As you visualize your character in various party situations, you may discover that your character is drinking a lot. Does that mean you are creating a character who is an alcoholic? To help you decide, consider the following. Below are some of the most common signs and symptoms of alcoholism. If you decide your character ought to be portrayed as an alcoholic, you'll want to employ several of these characteristic behaviors. (The below are generally accepted criteria gathered from a variety of sources.)

Signs and Symptoms of Alcoholism

• has five or more drinks a day
• tries to cut down or quit but fails
• feels uncomfortable if alcohol is not present at an event or function
• drinks while alone and prefers drinking alone
• hides the evidence of drinking
• experiences blackouts (periods of amnesia)
• uses alcohol to forget about worries or problems
• does things under the influence that are later regretted
• drinks much more than others in social situations

- neglects responsibilities in order to use alcohol
- experiences legal or financial troubles from using alcohol
- denies having any alcohol-related problems
- lies about alcohol use

Stages of Alcoholism

In some models, alcoholism is divided into three stages: early, middle, and late.

SOME EARLY-STAGE BEHAVIORS

- drinks heavily after a disappointment, quarrel, difficulty at work, or when under pressure
- grows a greater tolerance for alcohol consumption
- sneaks a few extra drinks at social situations

SOME MIDDLE-STAGE BEHAVIORS

- irritability when confronted about alcohol consumption
- begins switching brands or creating plans for controlling drinking
- avoids family and close friends while drinking

SOME LATE-STAGE BEHAVIORS

- eats very little or irregularly while drinking
- can't drink as much as before (liver problems)
- begins to have morning shakes and occasional hallucinations

Did You Know?

You can portray an alcoholic character who is not in recovery and who is also not drinking. A *dry drunk* is someone who by dint of will is currently not drinking but who in other ways is manifesting the traits of an alcoholic. She may be displaying reckless behavior, magical thinking (imagining that things can get done even though she is not attending to them), irresponsibility, and other traits associated with addiction, while at the same time managing to keep her hands off the booze.

Food for Thought

- Your alcoholic character has begun hiding bottles around the house. Her straight-laced mother arrives unannounced, begins straightening, and discovers her stash. How will she react?

• Your alcoholic character suffers from blackouts and can't remember one whole Saturday night of her life—the night she got married on a whim. How does this affect her self-image?

• After slamming her car into a tree, your alcoholic character goes to her first AA meeting. Describe the meeting.

SCENARIO NO. 6

STRANGER IN TOWN

A great way to investigate your character's personality is to imagine him in a new town, either having recently moved in or just passing through. This is not any old town, however: This is one of those sinister towns out of Westerns, spy movies, and horror movies—a town with a dark secret and an intense dislike of strangers. How would your character feel and act in such surroundings?

Get your character in mind and dream up the exact sort of town into which you'd like your character to venture. Will it be a small western town in the 1880s secretly run by a hold-up gang? Will it be a Polish town during World War II, where everyone is a potential collaborator and traitor? Will it be a medieval town in England where people die mysteriously and something strange is going on at the castle on the hill? Will it be a tight-knit, homogenous ethnic neighborhood where every newcomer is treated suspiciously? Will it be a border town where everyone has some kind of con game going? Consider what sort of town would make for the most interesting observations.

1. Your character notices that everyone is unfriendly. How does he react?

   A) Knowingly and without surprise, believing that people are generally exactly this unfriendly?

B) Knowingly but with some surprise, as this level of unfriendliness feels unprecedented?

c) With surprise and dismay?

D) With fear and anxiety?

E) With anger and reciprocal hostility?

•••

A) Reacting knowingly and without surprise is consistent with a cynical, world-wise, and world-weary character on the paranoid side—and perhaps with justification.

B) Reacting knowingly but with some surprise is consistent with an experienced, sensible character with good instincts who can recognize unusual hostility when he sees it.

c) Reacting with surprise and dismay is consistent with a naïve character who idealizes situations, tends to live in a fantasy world, and probably has trouble asking for what he wants and needs.

D) Reacting with fear and anxiety is a normal enough reaction that, if the reaction is very strong, is consistent with a character who has experienced a lot of trauma at the hands of society, perhaps as a member of a persecuted minority.

E) Reacting with anger and reciprocal hostility is consistent with a strong, fearless character who refuses to be beaten down by society and who is likely to manifest some heroic qualities if the situation demands it.

How does your character react to the fact that everyone in town is unfriendly?

•••••••••••••••••••••••••• 🤔 ••••••••••••••••••••••••••

2. Your character notices that people stop talking whenever he enters a public place. How does he start to enter public places?

A) Unobtrusively?

B) Matter-of-factly?

c) Flamboyantly?

D) Defiantly?

E) Rarely?

•••

A) Entering unobtrusively is consistent with an anxious character who either has been taught to accept whatever society dishes out and not make waves or who tends to live a secluded, isolated life and is generally uncomfortable in sticky social situations.

B) Entering matter-of-factly is consistent with a strong character who makes a point of not being pushed around, who may have some training in looking tough (like military service or police service), and who can be expected to act heroically if called upon to act.

c) Entering flamboyantly is consistent with a devil-may-care character who, perhaps because he is a member of a minority, is accustomed to marching into places where he is likely to receive a rude reception.

D) Entering defiantly is consistent with a character who likes to look in control but who is likely to crumble under real pressure or, alternatively, with a character who feels put upon and has taken too many blows in life and is ready to respond to attack with a hair trigger.

E) Entering rarely is consistent with a cautious character who would like to keep under the radar screen of society, who tends to keep to himself, and who sees discretion as the greater part of valor.

How does your character start to enter public places after he starts noticing that people fall silent upon his entrance?

3. Many suspicious things have happened and your character discovers that the key to his hotel room has suddenly stopped working. What is the first thing he does?

A) Report it to the front desk in a straightforward manner?
B) Report it to the front desk in a perplexed manner?
c) Report it to the front desk in an accusatory manner?
D) Report it to the front desk in a circumspect manner?
E) Report it to the front desk in a frightened manner?

A) Reporting the news in a straightforward manner is consistent with a tough-minded character who is not likely to believe in ghosts, not likely to run at the first sign of trouble, and not likely to back down from a fight.

B) Reporting the news in a perplexed manner is consistent with a naïve character who has some trouble with reality-testing, who tends to be taken by scam artists, and who may even make a habit of playing the fool.

C) Reporting the news in an accusatory manner is consistent with a character with a short fuse who expects to get what he pays for and who doesn't suffer fools gladly.

D) Reporting the news in a circumspect manner is consistent with an introspective character who likes to think through situations, who can be sly and devious when necessary, and who likes puzzles and mysteries.

E) Reporting the news in a frightened manner is consistent with an anxious character who may have suffered many traumas, including some significant recent ones, and who is likely to overreact to minor threats.

What is the first thing your character does when his key fails to unlock the door?

4. Your character is ending breakfast in a restaurant and someone at the next table utters a cryptic warning that he had better get out of town. What does your character do?

    A) Demand an explanation?
    B) Act as if he hasn't heard and go on eating breakfast, while churning inside?
    C) Act as if he hasn't heard and go on eating breakfast, while dismissing the message out-of-hand?
    D) Immediately pay the bill, leave the restaurant, and brood about the message?
    E) Immediately pay the bill, leave the restaurant, and leave the town?

A) Demanding an explanation is consistent with a powerful character who refuses to be intimidated or, alternatively, with a character with poor impulse control who regularly gets into confrontations.

B) Acting as if he hasn't heard while churning inside is consistent with a cautious, anxious character who is likely to manifest physical symptoms associated with anxiety, for example, stomach problems and headaches.

c) Acting as if he hasn't heard while dismissing the message is consistent with a strong character who is good at blocking out the negative in life or, alternatively, with an overly optimistic character who doesn't notice problems and who can easily be taken advantage of.

D) Leaving quickly and brooding about the message is consistent with a self-protective character who recognizes threats, thinks through ways of meeting them, and who may also anxiously obsess about the negatives in his life.

E) Leaving the restaurant and the town is consistent with a very prudent character who refuses to get enmeshed in the foolishness of others or, alternatively, with a jittery, fearful character who is easily intimidated.

What does your character do when he is issued a warning that he should get out of town?

5. Your character notices a new stranger in town—who, a day or two later, disappears. What does your character do?

    A) Presume that the stranger has simply left town?
    B) Make some informal inquiries?
    c) Begin to really investigate?
    D) Go to the police?
    E) Put the matter out of his mind?

A) Presuming that the stranger has simply left town is consistent with the reaction we would expect from the average person, who might wonder if something sinister had happened but who would dismiss that wonder as paranoid and melodramatic.

B) Making some informal inquiries is consistent with a character with time on his hands who may be bored and looking for a mystery to solve.

c) Beginning to really investigate is an unusual reaction consistent with a trained detective or a true busybody, as most people would find it imprudent to investigate and, equally importantly, wouldn't know how to begin to investigate.

D) Going to the police is consistent with a conventional, law-abiding, perhaps unimaginative character who, given all that is going on in this town, has naïvely failed to consider that the police may be part of the problem, not part of the solution.

E) Immediately leaving town is consistent with a very prudent character or, alternatively, with a frightened character who doesn't need to hear a second shoe drop to act and who is regularly startled by the sound of the first shoe dropping.

What does your character do when another stranger in town suddenly disappears?

6. Your character notices that all of the townspeople in this sinister town are gathering. What does your character do?

    A) Lock his door and stay inside?
    B) Join them to see what's happening?
    C) Follow them to surreptitiously see what's happening?
    D) Pack and ready himself to leave town?
    E) Pack and quickly leave town?

A) Locking the door and staying inside is consistent with a prudent character who knows his own basic powerlessness against a mob or, alternatively, with a fearful character who is too afraid to see what's happening or to get out of town.

B) Joining them to see what's happening is consistent with a brave character thumbing his nose in a gesture of defiance, or, alternatively, with a naïve character, possibly someone who has lived a pampered, sheltered life and doesn't recognize danger when it stares him in the face.

C) Following them to surreptitiously see what's happening is consistent with a solid, resourceful character who is brave enough to approach a mob but prudent enough to approach circumspectly.

D) Packing and getting ready to leave town is consistent with a character who recognizes danger but who may be slow to react and who may not get out of threatening situations in a timely manner.

E) Packing and quickly leaving town is consistent with a smart, sensible character who can clearly read the handwriting on the wall or, alternatively, with a timid character who flees too quickly and too often.

What does your character do when all the townspeople start gathering?

Situations to Consider

What would your character do if:

- The sheriff told him to get out of town?
- His belongings mysteriously disappeared out of his room?
- He found one of his car tires slashed?
- He found a listening device in his room?
- The waitress at the diner whispered to him, "You've got to help me!"?
- Townspeople took turns following him?
- A roadblock prevented him from leaving town?

Other Sinister Situations

Put your character in the most appropriate of the following situations and think through how he would act and react. If you like, flesh out the scene by adding one conflict and one surprise.

- your character's car breaks down next to a spooky castle
- your character is a spy behind enemy lines
- your character is on the run from the police
- your character rents a room in a strange boarding house
- your character is kidnapped and interrogated for information he doesn't possess
- your character returns to his hometown and nothing is as it was or should be
- your character starts work at a hospital where patients are mysteriously dying

The Stranger as Hero

One of the devices most often used by novelists and screenwriters is the hero's journey, a plot presumed to have archetypal resonance and employing certain more-or-less fixed elements. Very often the hero is a stranger in town—the hero-stranger rides into a troubled town, cleans it up, and wins the respect of the townsfolk and the love of the schoolmarm. Author and law professor James R. Elkins described the elements of the classic stranger-in-town plot on his "Lawyers & Film" Web site (http://myweb.wvnet.edu/~jelkins/film04/); among them are following:

- the hero is unknown to the society
- the hero is revealed to have an exceptional ability
- the society does not completely accept the hero
- the villains are stronger than the society; the society is weak
- the villains threaten the society
- the hero avoids involvement in the conflict
- the villains endanger a friend of the hero
- the hero fights the villains
- the hero defeats the villains
- the society accepts the hero

Imagine creating characters to populate a plotline of this sort. How would you make your characters feel new and fresh? What could you do to enliven the scared townsfolk, the principled schoolmarm, the cynical villain, and the hero himself? What would happen if the character you are currently investigating were dropped into this classic plot? Would he fit the bill or stick out like a sore thumb?

Did You Know?

A relationship that frequently appears in the hero's journey plot is the hero-mentor one. Elkins explained:

> The relationship between hero and mentor is one of the most common themes in mythology. It stands for the bond between parent and child, teacher and student, doctor and patient, god and man.

Imagine the character you're investigating functioning as a mentor. Who, if anyone, would he be likely to mentor? What sort of mentor would he make?

Food for Thought

• When you visualize your character in harm's way in one or another of these sinister situations, do you see him as more rising to the occasion or more turning to jelly?

• Stranger in town is a metaphor for the individual separated from—and often at odds with—society at large. To what extent is your character alienated from his culture and society? On a scale from 1 to 10, 10 being the most alienated, what score would you give your character?

• In what sorts of towns (rural towns in the South, villages in Wales, ethnic neighborhoods in big cities, etc.) would your character feel most like a stranger and in which would he feel least like a stranger?

SCENARIO NO. 7

FLIRTING

Who doesn't flirt sometimes? Imagine your character in a bar and in a flirting mood. Picture a bar that will best help you investigate your character: a jumping urban bar late at night, a honky-tonk bar with live bluegrass music, a sedate wood-and-leather hotel bar, a crowded London wine bar, a dive off the highway in the middle of nowhere. Where would you like your character to do her flirting?

Populate the bar with an interesting mix of characters and some attractive guys or gals eager to do some flirting themselves. Get the energy level of the bar clearly in mind: spring break wild, airport bar busy but anonymous, early evening half-dead? Picture your character entering, choosing a spot to sit, looking around, ordering a drink, and settling in for a little innocent flirting.

1. What does your character order?

   A) A glass of wine?
   B) A beer?
   C) A fruit-flavored margarita?
   D) The latest cocktail?
   E) A whiskey?

Drinks and stereotypes go together—as for instance the stereotype of the San Francisco football fan sipping white wine at football games rather than guzzling good, old-fashioned beer. You can use stereotypes to your advantage, marking your character as clearly from a particular social class or educational background, or you can play against stereotype, having your working-class stiff order fine wine or your petite heroine throwing back bourbons.

A) Ordering a glass of wine is consistent with a college-educated, urban and urbane character of the professional class.

B) Ordering a beer is consistent with a conventional, working class character who is likely to lean toward the right on political and social issues.

C) Ordering a fruit-flavored margarita is consistent with a party animal who likes to fly to Mexican hot spots for spring break, who dreams of Mardi Gras in New Orleans and Rio, and who rarely stops at one drink—or two or three.

D) Ordering the latest cocktail is consistent with a hip, sophisticated character—or someone who wants to appear hip and sophisticated—who is affluent enough to spring for the elevated prices of fashionable drinks.

E) Ordering a whiskey is consistent with a hard-drinking character who is likely on the hardened side and who has seen her share of life—perhaps from the bottom of a bottle.

What drink does your character order?

2. An attractive someone makes eye contact with your character. What is the first thing she does?

   A) Look away quickly?
   B) Meet the glance briefly, then look away?
   C) Meet the glance in a lingering way, then look away?
   D) Smile and nod?
   E) March right over?

A) Looking away quickly is consistent with a shy character who lets lots of life's opportunities pass by and who is similarly likely to experience a lot of regret over her missed opportunities.

B) Meeting the glance briefly, then looking away, is consistent with a character who, although on the shy side, has enough self-confidence to reciprocate a glance and who is likely to come back for a second glance.

c) Meeting the glance in a lingering way, then looking away, is consistent with a self-confident character who perhaps has a lot on her mind or, alternatively, with a self-confident character who is playing a studied role of casualness.

· D) Smiling and nodding is consistent with a friendly, extroverted character who takes easily to new people and who may pop up and visit if another glance is exchanged.

E) Marching right over is consistent with a powerful character high in energy and sex appeal or, alternatively, with a weak character who is used to disguising that weakness through bold gestures.

What is the first thing your character does when an attractive someone makes eye contact?

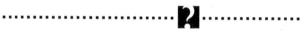

3. When your character looks over a second time, the attractive stranger is staring right at her. What does your character do?

    A) Blush and quickly look away?
    B) Return the stare?
    c) Don an enough-is-enough expression?
    D) Calmly look away?
    E) Join the other person?

A) Blushing and quickly looking away is consistent with a shy character who is likely to experience severe enough performance anxiety that she will be hampered occupationally and socially.

B) Returning the stare is consistent with a confident character who, because she can be intrigued and remain calm at the same time, is likely good at intellectual and creative work.

c) Donning an enough-is-enough expression is consistent with a mercurial, sour personality, somebody whose enthusiasms and passions pass quickly, leaving anger or depression in their wake.

D) Calmly looking away is consistent with a character who is confident but who, perhaps because she is in a committed relationship, has decided to end the flirtation at this innocent juncture.

E) Joining the other person is consistent with a confident person, someone who is able to take action, and who is probably ambitious and most likely successful in the world.

What would your character do if, glancing back a second time, she found the attractive stranger staring?

4. How often would your character be the one to initiate the flirting?

   A) Never?
   B) Rarely?
   C) A lot of the time?
   D) Most of the time?
   E) All of the time?

A) If your character would never initiate the flirting, that is consistent with a constipated character with puritan tendencies and, quite likely, some obsessive-compulsive habits, as, for instance, a too-neat underwear drawer.

B) If your character would only rarely initiate the flirting, that is consistent with a character who has been harmed in the interpersonal arena and raised in a loveless environment but who has retained enough of a spark to occasionally flirt.

C) If your character would initiate the flirting a lot of the time, that is consistent with a character with healthy appetites and the courage to risk who possesses enough restraint and moderation not to flirt wantonly or inappropriately.

D) If your character would initiate the flirting most of the time, that is consistent with a character who is likely to find monogamous relating difficult and who might remain loyal while at home but stray on every business trip.

E) If your character would initiate the flirting all the time, that is consistent with a character obsessed with sex who is likely promiscuous, unfaithful, and probably addicted to more than sex.

How often would your character be the one to initiate the flirting?

5. Your character glances up and sees that the other person is approaching and means to join her. What is her reaction (presuming that she finds the other person attractive)?

    A) Terror?
    B) Significant panic?
    C) A mild case of nerves?
    D) Excitement?
    E) Indifference?

A) Reacting with terror is consistent with a sheltered character with low self-esteem and a poor self-image who has experienced victimization in interpersonal and sexual relationships.

B) Reacting with significant panic is consistent with a character whose façade is easily pierced, who likely plays second banana to her friends, and who feels awkward in most if not all social situations.

C) Reacting with a mild case of nerves—perhaps a mixture of anxiety and excitement—is probably the most usual reaction and consistent with a character with healthy appetites, natural concerns, and a willingness to engage in the give-and-take of romance.

D) Reacting with pure excitement is consistent with a playful, ebullient character who is likely to have problems with impulse control and may get into a lot of messes and fixes.

E) Reacting with indifference is consistent with a character who is genuinely bored, rarely experiences pleasure, and is probably depressed, or, alternatively, with a character who is posing as bored so as to make a cool impression.

How would your character react to an attractive stranger joining her?

6. Your character has been flirting with someone across the room, glances up, and sees that the other person has left. How does your character react?

A) With relief?
B) With annoyance?
C) With anger?
D) With irony?
E) With indifference?

• •

A) Reacting with relief is consistent with a certain shyness, inexperience, and lack of confidence or, alternatively, with an unconscious dislike of people in general or sexual dynamics in particular.

B) Reacting with annoyance is consistent with a character who regularly feels that she misses the boat, fails to grasp opportunities, and sees herself as unlucky in love and in life.

C) Reacting with anger is consistent with a volatile, perhaps violent character who overreacts to rejection, possesses unhealthy narcissistic tendencies, and rapidly cycles relationships.

D) Reacting with irony is consistent with an intellectual character who finds it amusing that a nicely charged flirtation can end in the blink of an eye, leaving in its wake an accustomed void.

E) Reacting with indifference is consistent with a character who is less interested in sex and romance than she lets on, who is generally passive and unenthusiastic, and whose relationships are characterized by their dullness.

How would your character react if the other person suddenly left?

Situations to Consider

What would your character do if:

• Someone inappropriately came on to your character?

• Someone accused your character of flirting when she really wasn't?

• She was just coming out of a long-term relationship and preparing for the dating scene?

• She was given a present of a book with flirting instructions?

• Someone she had always considered just a friend began flirting with her?

• Two people began flirting with her?

• Your character suddenly felt unattractive?

Other Flirting Situations

Put your character in the most appropriate of the following situations and think through how she would act and react. If you like, flesh out the scene by adding one conflict and one surprise.

- flirting in a foreign country
- flirting at a wedding
- flirting in the dark during a power outage
- flirting while high
- flirting while sober
- flirting with someone of a different race
- flirting at the office

How the Modern Woman Flirts

How does the modern woman flirt? In a *Psychology Today* magazine article titled "The New Flirting Game," author Deborah Lott observed:

> Psychologist Monica Moore of Webster University has spent more than 2,000 hours observing women flirting maneuvers in restaurants, singles bars and at parties. According to her findings, women give non-verbal cues that get a flirtation rolling fully two-thirds of the time. Moore tallied a total of 52 different nonverbal courtship behaviors used by women, including glancing, gazing (short and sustained), primping, preening, smiling, lip licking, pouting, giggling, laughing and nodding.

How does the character you're investigating flirt? Can you identify three or four behaviors that your character possesses in her repertoire of flirting behaviors?

Did You Know?

Do young girls flirt the same way that older women do? Lott explained:

> In observations of 100 girls between the ages of 13 and 16 at shopping malls, ice skating rinks and other places adolescents congregate, Moore found the teens exhibiting 31 of the 52 courtship signals deployed by adult women. Overall, the teens' gestures looked less natural than ones made by mature

females: they laughed more boisterously and preened more obviously, and their moves were broader and rougher.

Food for Thought

• Is your character likely or unlikely to flirt? What does that say about her personality or self-image?

• If your character were in a significant, committed relationship, would she still flirt? If so, where would she draw the line?

• When is your character most likely to flirt and when is she least likely to flirt?

SCENARIO NO. 8

AT THE AIRPORT

Your character finds himself with a few hours to kill at the airport. On the surface, nothing much goes on during those dead hours as passengers grab a snack, watch sports at the bar, read a book or a magazine, do business on their laptop, or stare into space. Yet each person is exactly himself as he waits, and a trained eye—yours—can catch nuances of personality in the way this person bellies up to the airport bar and has his cell phone glued to his ear the whole time.

Picture your character in a busy airport between flights with two hours to kill. How will he pass the time? More telling still, what will he be *thinking*? This is an opportunity to imagine your character's inner life during an undramatic, tedious wait between flights.

1. What is your character's basic attitude as he waits? Is he:

   A) Restless?
   B) Busy?
   C) Blank?
   D) Thoughtful?
   E) Observant?

A) Waiting restlessly is consistent with a Type A character whose appetites, ambitions, and high energy level make it impossible for him to relax.

B) Keeping busy is consistent with a defended character who finds his own inner life dangerous and who keeps busy to avoid the silence of stopping or, alternatively, with a character under such workload pressure that he must work every waking minute of the day.

C) Waiting blankly is consistent with a conventional, socialized character who is not in the habit of using his spare time as a time to think.

D) Spending his time in thought is consistent with an intellectual character who may be an artist or a professional and who attempts to solve intellectual puzzles or pursue his creative ideas as he waits.

E) Spending his time observing is consistent with a character who is a trained observer, like a visual artist or a policeman, or, alternatively, with an ironic character who takes pleasure in watching the foibles of the human race unfold as he waits.

What is your character's basic attitude as he waits?

2. A family with whiny children sits down next to your character. What does he do?

    A) Continue reading his book or magazine?
    B) Watch their antics with an amused air?
    C) Watch their antics with an annoyed air?
    D) Strike up a conversation?
    E) Move?

A) Continuing to read is consistent with a stoic character who has decided to take life's little difficulties in stride or, alternatively, with a thoughtful character so engrossed in his own thoughts that he doesn't notice the commotion.

B) Watching their antics with an amused air is consistent with a character who is a parent himself and who enjoys the antics of children, even at their whiniest (just so long as he doesn't have to take someone else's whiny children home with him).

c) Watching their antics with an annoyed air is consistent with a critical, self-absorbed character who likes to make his displeasure known when something isn't working or when someone isn't behaving up to his standards.

D) Striking up a conversation is consistent with a friendly, socialized character who is in the habit of engaging in superficial chatter with the people he meets or, alternatively, with a lonely character whose few human contacts consist of brief encounters of this sort.

E) Moving is consistent with a matter-of-fact character who is in the habit of taking decisive action the instant action is called for or, alternatively, with a passive-aggressive character who, without saying anything, manages to communicate his displeasure to the unruly children's parents.

How would your character react to the arrival of a family with whiny children?

3. Your character notices an unattended piece of luggage. What does he do?

 A) Watch to see if its owner returns?
 B) Immediately call airport security?
 C) Wait several minutes before calling airport security?
 D) Leave the area, but feel guilty for leaving?
 E) Leave the area, and put the matter out of his mind?

A) Watching to see if the owner returns is consistent with a wary character who intends to do the right thing but who, weighing inconveniencing a fellow passenger against the potential safety risk, is conflicted about what constitutes the right thing to do in these circumstances.

B) Immediately calling airport security is consistent with a nervous, socialized character who takes the messages that come over airport loudspeakers literally or, alternatively, with a trained professional who is accustomed to reacting instantly to possible danger.

C) Waiting several minutes before calling security is consistent with a thoughtful, decisive character who understands that there is a difference between a bag left unattended for a few minutes by a forgetful passenger who has gone to the rest room and a bag left completely unattended.

D) Leaving the area but feeling guilty about leaving is consistent with a passive, anxious character who knows the difference between right and wrong but who doesn't feel emotionally or psychologically able to step up to the plate and do the right thing.

E) Leaving the area and putting the matter out of his mind is consistent with a self-absorbed character too busy with his own life to entertain empathic thoughts or, alternatively, with an optimistic character who is not inclined to find anything sinister or dangerous about an unattended suitcase.

What would your character do if he noticed an unattended piece of luggage?

4. As your character waits, what is primarily on his mind?

   A) Work?
   B) Home?
   C) Sex?
   D) Money?
   E) Ideas?

A) Having work on the mind is consistent with a Type A character who is likely driven in life and glued to his cell phone or his computer screen the whole time he finds himself waiting in airports.

B) Having home on the mind is consistent with a family-oriented character who finds traveling burdensome or, alternatively, with a fearful character who is anxious about traveling and finds security in conjuring up images of home.

C) Having sex on the mind is consistent with an appetitive character who is likely to end up at the airport bar or the airport restaurant because such a place is able to satisfy at least some of his appetitive needs.

D) Having money on the mind is consistent with an ambitious, greedy character who spends his time learning what things cost, how they can be had cheaply, how they can be sold for a profit, and how he can get one over on people.

E) Having ideas on the mind is consistent with a thoughtful, perhaps intellectual and artistic character who relishes the anonymity of airports and who perhaps does some of his best thinking while traveling.

What is primarily on your character's mind as he waits?

5. Your character's flight is delayed at the last minute just before boarding, but no information about the reason for the delay or the length of the delay is provided. How long would your character wait before marching up to the counter and asking questions?

  A) Would he march up instantly?
  B) Would he wait five minutes?
  C) Would he wait ten minutes?
  D) Would he wait fifteen minutes?
  E) Would he continue waiting without asking?

A) Marching up instantly is consistent with an assertive character who is perhaps also abrasive and bullying and who is quick to make his displeasure known when things go wrong and people fail him.

B) Waiting five minutes is consistent with a self-assured character who is happy to give people the benefit of a doubt but who also believes that others ought to act responsibly, for instance, by making an announcement when a delay occurs.

C) Waiting ten minutes is consistent with a character so absorbed in his own thoughts that he hardly notices the delay but who, once he notices it, is self-confident enough to hop up and inquire.

D) Waiting fifteen minutes is consistent with a socialized, conventional character who is inclined to take his time before making waves and who is likely to make waves gently if and when he does make them.

E) Waiting indefinitely is consistent with a passive, anxious character who is a victim of learned helplessness or, alternatively, with a phlegmatic character who actually doesn't care when the flight will leave.

How would your character react to a delay accompanied by no information?

6. Does your character's mood change as the boarding commences?

   A) Does he become nervous?
   B) Does he become passive?
   C) Does he become enthusiastic?
   D) Does he become hostile?
   E) Does he experience no particular change?

A) Becoming nervous is consistent with a phobic character who has a fear of flying and whose panic grows as the boarding process commences.

B) Becoming passive is consistent with a conventional, socialized character who turns himself over to the control and authority of the system once he enters any sort of line.

C) Becoming enthusiastic is consistent with a passionate, optimistic character who enjoys flying, always reserves a window seat, and can't wait for the views from 30,000 feet in the air.

D) Becoming significantly more restless is consistent with a character who dislikes losing control and the feeling of inhibited flight that sitting in a tight airplane seat with your seat belt buckled provokes.

E) Experiencing no particular change is consistent with a character who is a seasoned traveler and who flies so often that he takes these routines for granted or, alternatively, with a phlegmatic character who takes no notice of whether he is on the ground or 30,000 feet above it.

How does your character's mood change as the time for boarding approaches?

Situations to Consider

What would your character do if:

- The airport had to be evacuated?
- His flight was canceled?
- An attractive stranger struck up a conversation?
- He spotted an acquaintance sitting on the other side of the terminal?
- A blind person asked for help getting to the restroom?

• The book he was reading was missing its last page?

• The television reported an airplane crash?

Other Waiting Situations

Put your character in the most appropriate of the following situations and think through how he would act and react. If you like, flesh out the scene by adding one conflict and one surprise.

• at the dentist
• in line at the Department of Motor Vehicles
• in a foreign bank
• at a seedy bus station
• at the opera, before the curtain rises
• at a job interview
• in traffic

Waiting and Anxiety

Your character is on a long line leading to the security screening checkpoint. The line isn't moving. How does he react? According to author and consultant David Maister in an article titled "The Psychology of Waiting Lines," almost everyone in a situation of this sort reacts with some level of anxiety. Maister explained that this anxiety is reduced if the officials involved provide relevant information:

> On a recent Eastern Airlines shuttle flight with open seating, my fellow passengers formed an agitated queue at the boarding gate, leading the attendant to announce: "Don't worry, folks, the plane's a big one; you'll all get on." The change in atmosphere in the waiting lounge was remarkable. Similar efforts to deal with customer anxiety can be seen when airlines make on-board announcements that connecting flights are being held for a delayed flight.

Every person is anxious sometimes. How does you character manifest his anxiety? Picture your character in a line that just will not move. What does you character look like from the outside? What is going on inside?

Did You Know?

People experience waits of a known length, even if they are very long, with less difficulty and less anxiety than waits where the length of the wait is unknown, even if that wait ultimately proves quite short. Maister explained:

Patients who arrive early for an appointment will sit contentedly until the scheduled time, even if this is a significant amount of time in an absolute sense (say, thirty minutes). However, once the appointment time is passed, even a short wait of, say, ten minutes, grows increasingly annoying, as this waiting has no knowable limit.

Bring your character to mind. How does he wait when the wait is of a known length? How does he wait when the appointment time passes and no one tells him how long the wait will last?

Food for Thought

• On a scale of 1 to 10, 10 being the most agitated, how agitated does your character get as he waits?

• Which waiting situations provoke the most agitation in your character and which provoke the least?

• To what lengths, if any, does your character go so as to not have to wait?

SCENARIO NO. 9

NEW NEIGHBORS

Imagine the neighborhood in which your character lives (this may be different for each character you investigate). Try to picture it clearly, going up and down its streets in your mind's eye, getting a mental picture of its schools, churches, shopping areas, and so on. Is it urban, suburban, rural? Is it a neighborhood in a big city that feels like a secluded enclave? Is it a small town whose main street is a fast highway flanked by gas stations and fast food joints? Is it a different country and/or a different time: Prague of today or Prague of 1840, Greenwich Village of today or Greenwich Village of 1920?

Once you have your character's neighborhood clearly in mind, ask yourself, "What sort of couple or family would be least likely to move in next door to my character?" Some examples are a young couple moving into a neighborhood of retirees, a biker family moving into an upscale suburban neighborhood, or a suburban family moving into a rough-and-tumble inner city neighborhood. Get your character's new neighbors clearly in mind and then proceed.

1. When your character looks out the window and sees his new neighbors moving in, what are his first thoughts?

A) "What are they doing here?"
B) "How interesting that they chose this neighborhood!"
c) "I'd like to get to know them."
D) "I hope they keep to themselves."
E) "That one looks attractive."

A) Thinking "What are they doing here?" is consistent with an intellectual character who is genuinely curious about his neighbors' choice or, alternatively, with a prejudiced character who is territorial, small-minded, and generally critical.

B) Thinking "How interesting that they chose this neighborhood!" is consistent with a character with a sense of humor and a whimsical nature who is amused by life's oddities, including people making bewildering choices as to where to live.

c) Thinking "I'd like to get to know them," is consistent with a character who is genuinely open, compassionate, and good-natured, and who might get romantically involved with someone very different from himself.

D) Thinking "I hope they keep to themselves," is consistent with a close-minded character who may publicly express tolerant beliefs but whose true bigoted attitudes are likely to leak out at the least provocation—or with no provocation at all.

E) Thinking "That one looks attractive," is consistent with a character who, even if prejudiced and close-minded, is nevertheless more interested in sex and romance than in his own biases.

What are your character's first thoughts when he looks out the windows and sees his new neighbors?

2. Your character hears a knock at the door, goes to the door, and looks through the peephole. There, outside, is one of his new neighbors. Does he:

A) Open the door a crack?
B) Open the door wide in a friendly manner?
c) Open the door wide in an aggressive manner?

D) Stay there silently without opening the door?
E) Turn around and withdraw?

A) Opening the door a crack is consistent with an anxious character who is likely to open the door a crack, metaphorically speaking, in the rest of his life as well, venturing into new territories and new ideas only timidly and reluctantly—if at all.

B) Opening the door wide in a friendly manner is consistent with an extroverted, sociable character who is open to new experiences and people and who possesses a wide circle of friends and an even wider circle of acquaintances.

C) Opening the door wide in an aggressive manner is consistent with an oppositional character who is probably bullying and maybe violent, who claims to know his own mind, and whose short fuse makes him the bane of clerks and customer service representatives.

D) Staying there silently without opening the door is consistent with a character of two minds in life, someone with simmering dynamic inner conflicts who might, in the next second, fling the door open, perhaps because friendliness or civility has won, or walk quickly away, because prejudice or isolationism has won.

E) Turning around and withdrawing is consistent with a character who has learned how to mind his business and finds discretion a prudent way of life or, alternatively, with a prejudiced character whose biases run so wide and deep that even a moment's conversation at the door is out the question.

What does your character do after looking through the peephole?

3. Your character invites his new neighbor in and they chat. Is your character:

A) Inquisitive?
B) Interrogative?
C) Self-revealing?
D) Extra-friendly?
E) Cool and distanced?

A) An inquisitive attitude is consistent with a friendly, open, and curious character who has traveled extensively and has a wide experience of the world or, alternatively, with a character who is a member of a culture that values open and friendly interactions with neighbors.

B) An interrogative attitude is consistent with a character who is tough-minded, unafraid to say what's on his mind, and used to taking charge in interpersonal situations.

C) A self-revealing attitude is consistent with a naïve, innocent character or, alternatively, with a character with inappropriate boundaries who gets too close too quickly to the people he meets.

D) Acting extra-friendly is consistent with a compensatory reaction (like liberal guilt) where a person endeavors not to look biased, even if he really is, or, alternatively, with a calculating reaction meant to disarm and deceive.

E) Acting cool and distanced is consistent with a cautious character who plays life close to the vest, withholds information in most situations, and is likely on the sour, critical, and, perhaps, depressed side.

What is your character's attitude during this conversation?

4. The new neighbor makes a reference that your character doesn't understand. Does he think:

A) "Those people!"
B) "I'm so ignorant!"
C) "How interesting!"
D) "How suspicious!"
E) "Should I ask what he meant?"

A) Thinking "Those people!" is consistent with an intolerant character whose first reaction is to blame others for his problems and failures.

B) Thinking "I'm so ignorant!" is consistent with a self-disparaging character who manifests low self-esteem, a timid personality, and an unwillingness to go after his dreams.

c) Thinking "How interesting!" is consistent with an open character who finds life fascinating, believes in lifelong learning, and is likely well educated and widely read.

d) Thinking "How suspicious!" is consistent with a paranoid character who is likely a conspiracy buff and simultaneously skeptical and naïve—for instance, skeptical about governmental explanations regarding UFOs but naively accepting of UFO sightings.

e) Thinking "Should I ask what he meant?" is consistent with a timid character burdened by anxieties who regularly second-guesses himself.

How does your character react to a reference that he doesn't understand?

5. The new neighbor invites your character to come over for a visit some evening. Does your character:

    a) Instantly accept?
    b) Reluctantly accept?
    c) Accept but back out later?
    d) Diplomatically refuse?
    e) Curtly refuse?

a) Instantly accepting is consistent with an impulsive character; with a weak character who can't say no; or with a friendly, sociable, and perhaps happy-go-lucky character who is genuinely interested in visiting.

b) Reluctantly accepting is consistent with a character who bends to social pressures and is relatively unable to set his own agenda in life, instead being pulled by social norms and conventions.

c) Accepting but backing out later is consistent with a character who has a hard time saying no in face-to-face situations or, alternatively, with a savvy character who finds it useful to act agreeably in the moment and then make up his mind at leisure.

d) Diplomatically refusing is consistent with a character with professional graces who is careful with time commitments and may even be so busy that he has trouble making time for intimates and close friends.

E) Curtly refusing is consistent with an intolerant character who either lacks social graces or who feels justified in acting rudely whenever it suits him.

How does your character react to the invitation?

6. Your character looks out the window and sees his neighbor in some trouble. Does your character:

A) Rush out to help?
B) Reluctantly help?
C) Dial 911?
D) Do nothing, but feel guilty?
E) Do nothing, period?

A) Rushing out to help is consistent with a principled, courageous, and altruistic character who is likely to act heroically in a wide variety of situations.

B) Reluctantly helping is consistent with a character torn between principle and self-protection who is principled enough to act even when he would prefer to turn away.

C) Dialing 911 is consistent with a character who is inclined to do the right thing and who quite possibly can be counted on in tough situations, especially if he can act anonymously.

D) Doing nothing and subsequently feeling guilty is consistent with a weak character plagued by anxiety and doubt who knows the difference between right and wrong but doesn't feel emotionally or physically equal to standing on principle.

E) Doing nothing, period, is consistent with a character who is set in his bigotry, inclined to divide the world into us vs. them categories, and even an active participant in prejudiced behaviors.

What would your character do if his new neighbor needed help?

Situations to Consider

What would your character do if:

• The town rallied against the new neighbors?

• The new neighbors asked your character for a big favor?
• The new neighbors came to your character's home to hide from a mob?
• The new neighbors shunned your character?
• The new neighbors turned aggressive toward your character?
• The new neighbors ran down their property?
• Your character moved and became the new neighbor?

Other Difference Situations

Put your character in the most appropriate of the following situations and think through how he would act and react. If you like, flesh out the scene by adding one conflict and one surprise.

• spending an academic year abroad
• visiting an old buddy who has struck it rich
• visiting an old buddy who is now down and out
• traveling on business to an exotic locale
• discovering that his new in-laws are of a different social class
• participating in a religious ceremony not his own
• spending a weekend among people with different political ideas

The Stereotypical American

The new neighbors scenario investigates how your character constructs and reacts to stereotypes. But how, in turn, is he seen? How, for instance, is the typical or stereotypical American viewed by other cultures?

It makes sense to think through to what extent your character, if he is an American, runs or doesn't run true to stereotypical form. The following are twenty qualities, some positive, some negative, frequently associated with the typical American. How does your character stack up?

outgoing	friendly
informal	loud
rude	boastful
immature	hard working
wealthy	generous
extravagant	wasteful
opinionated	cocksure
disrespectful of authority	racially prejudiced

ignorant of other countries	time conscious
in a rush	promiscuous

To what extent does your character share these qualities? Do you want him to partake of more or fewer of them, so as to make him more or less of a cultural stereotype?

Did You Know?

Characters in novels tend not to move a lot, but people in real life do. According to the Census Bureau, in the 1950s and 1960s about one in five American adults moved annually. In recent years, people have been moving from one residence to another less frequently, the number declining to about one in six in 2000. That still means that 15 percent of the adult population in America changes their address annually. Does that reality have a place in your novel?

Food for Thought

• This scenario gives you the chance to get your character's socioeconomic status, academic background, religious persuasion, ethnic identification, and other social and cultural aspects of character clearly in mind. Paint a social portrait of your character.

• As a rule, is your character tolerant or intolerant?

• Is your character tolerant with respect to certain groups and certain differences, and intolerant with respect to other groups and other differences? Can you identify these differences?

SCENARIO NO. 10
BLOWING THE WHISTLE

At one time or another everyone learns information that, if revealed, might cost her something important—her job, her physical safety, the respect of her peers. A person may learn that her boss is embezzling, that the product she is manufacturing has a dangerous design flaw, that her pastor or rabbi is sleeping around, and so on.

In this scenario, imagine that your character is working at a company that manufactures a product and that she discovers there are safety problems. Also imagine that your character has a lot to lose by blowing the whistle—for the sake of this scenario, picture her with children in school, a hefty mortgage to pay, many social connections among her peers at the company, and so on. When you have both the importance of the problem and the importance of not blowing the whistle clearly in mind, proceed to answer the following questions.

1. What is the first thing your character does upon learning of the safety problem?

   A) Grow anxious, knowing that this is going to be a big problem no matter what?

   B) Immediately take the matter to a superior?

c) Discuss the matter privately with a peer?

D) Mentally and emotionally prepare to blow the whistle, presuming that no action is going to be taken?

E) Put it out of her head?

•••

A) Growing anxious because she knows that this is a going to be a big deal is consistent with a self-aware character who realizes she is going to experience pangs of conscience if she doesn't report the problem and real consequences if she does report it, and that there's no easy way out of the dilemma.

B) Immediately taking the matter to a superior is consistent with a character on the subservient side who prefers to pass the buck or, alternatively, with a character who is fearless, quick to act, and presumes that people in the organization will do their job and do the right thing.

c) Discussing the matter privately with a peer is consistent with a cautious character who needs to enlist support before taking difficult action or, alternatively, with a savvy character who wants a second opinion about whether the problem is as serious as it appears.

D) Presuming that no action will be taken and readying herself to blow the whistle is consistent with a skeptical, perhaps cynical character who supposes that people only rarely rise to the occasion or act in principled ways.

E) Putting it out of her head is consistent with a conventional, socialized character who is good at denying reality and is likely to act defensively in her personal interactions and business dealings.

What is the first thing your character does upon learning of the safety problem?

••••••••••••••••••••••••••  ••••••••••••••••••••••••••

2. Your character is toying with the idea of blowing the whistle. What will help make up her mind?

A) If another person agrees to come forward?

B) If, in discussing the matter with her mate, she feels supported?

c) If, upon reflection, the problem seems just too serious to ignore?

D) If she feels legally liable and exposed?

E) If the product fails and someone is injured or killed?

•••

A) Needing another person to come forward before blowing the whistle is consistent with a conventional character who is unlikely to take heroic action in any sphere of her life and who is easily influenced by group taste and group ideals.

B) First discussing the matter with her mate is consistent with a character who treats her relationships seriously and considers it a matter of principle to check in before embarking on anything potentially dangerous or, alternatively, with a weak character who lives life more as a follower than a leader.

C) Arriving at the feeling that the matter is just too serious to ignore is consistent with a thoughtful, introspective character with solid principles who may not act hastily but who acts decisively once she decides to act.

D) Blowing the whistle because of a fear of legal liability is consistent with a timid character afraid of all of her alternatives, or, alternatively, with a savvy character who recognizes that her legal liabilities are a graver danger than possibly losing her job.

E) Only reporting the problem after someone gets injured or killed is consistent with an indecisive character who is motivated less by principle than by emotion and who probably waits too long in other areas of her life as well—for instance, getting out of bad jobs and bad relationships.

What will help your character make up her mind to blow the whistle?

3. Your character reports the problem to a superior and is told to forget about it. What does your character do?

- A) Forget about it without any qualms?
- B) Forget about it but with a guilty conscience?
- C) Take the matter to a higher-ranking superior?
- D) Feel uncertain about what to do next and adopt a wait-and-see attitude?
- E) Make a record of the conversation, photocopy files, and ready herself to blow the whistle?

A) Forgetting about it without a qualm is consistent with a character who defers to authority, prefers taking orders to affirming principles, and is probably conventional in most of her behaviors and beliefs.

B) Forgetting about it with some pangs of conscience is consistent with a character who is thoughtful and introspective enough to understand moral distinctions but insufficiently strong to take action and stand on principle.

C) Taking the matter to a higher-ranking superior is consistent with a character who is strong-minded but also a believer in institutions and the idea of chain-of-command, someone who makes a good—if perhaps naïve—team player.

D) Adopting a wait-and-see attitude is consistent with a passive character who is probably indecisive and unenthusiastic in other aspects of her life, someone likely to wait too long to begin projects, achieve goals, and fulfill dreams.

E) Readying herself to blow the whistle is consistent with a strong, principled, thoughtful character who is likely to have acted heroically in the past and who prefers to keep her own counsel on matters of importance.

What does your character do when told to forget about the problem?

4. Your character decides not to report the problem. How does she react to that decision?

    A) With a lot of guilt?
    B) With a little guilt?
    C) With a rationalization?
    D) With some anxiety about being found out?
    E) Without batting an eye?

A) Reacting with a lot of guilt is consistent with a character who regularly fails herself and then follows up her failures with deep-seated, simmering regrets, creating an enduring dynamic of depression.

B) Reacting with a little guilt is consistent with a weak, conventional character who has received enough lessons about right and wrong to know that her response is inadequate but who isn't self-directing or self-confident enough to act on principle.

C) Reacting with a rationalization or some other defense mechanism is consistent with a character who lacks self-awareness, blames others before she blames herself, and is adept at avoiding taking responsibility for the consequences of her actions.

D) Reacting with anxiety about being found out is consistent with a fearful character in whom trust would be misplaced, someone who can be expected to act deviously and whose main concern is for her own safety.

E) Not blowing the whistle and then not batting an eye is consistent with a character without a conscience, someone who knows how to conspire, get ahead, and operate in groups and who is highly ambitious and quite likely successful in business—though not in relationships.

How does your character react to her decision not to blow the whistle?

5. Your character does not blow the whistle. Then there is a fatal accident involving the product. What does your character do now?

A) Go to her superiors?
B) Go to a peer in the company?
C) Consult a lawyer?
D) Nothing, but with increased guilty feelings?
E) Nothing, with no guilty feelings?

A) Going to her superiors after a fatal accident involving the product is consistent with a worried, perhaps naïve character who is looking less for answers than reassurance or, alternatively, with a character with enough backbone that a fatality finally provokes some action.

B) Going to a peer in the company after a fatal accident is consistent with a character who needs support in standing up to power and who is probably not going to take any action in the matter, as her peer is not likely to encourage whistle-blowing or any radical action.

C) Consulting a lawyer is consistent with a careful, perhaps savvy character who is used to weighing her options and choices and who may proceed to take action if, and only if, she can get her ducks lined up in a row.

D) Doing nothing, but with an increase in guilty feelings, is consistent with a passive, defeated character who possesses a conscience but not the wherewithal to take independent action or bear up to the consequences of independent action.

E) Doing nothing and experiencing no guilt is consistent with a conventional character who looks out for herself and who is practiced at making moral pronouncements, pointing the finger at others, and in general acting hypocritically.

After a fatal accident involving the product, what does your character do?

6. Your character blows the whistle and an excuse is found to fire her. What is your character's reaction? Is she:

A) Angry, but takes no action?
B) Angry, and takes legal or other action?
C) Upset at herself?
D) More anxious at being unemployed than upset or angry?
E) Philosophical and phlegmatic?

A) Feeling anger but taking no action is consistent with a character who feels impotent in life, who sees power and control residing in the hands of others, and who may allow her anger to build up until it explodes in some inappropriate way or at some inappropriate target.

B) Feeling anger and taking action is consistent with a powerful, self-confident character who refuses to be pushed around or, alternatively, with a less self-confident character who is pushed by this particular and extreme set of circumstances to finally take a stand.

C) Feeling upset with herself is consistent with a self-critical, self-flagellating character who, out of weakness and anxiety, tends to blame herself while letting those actually to blame off the hook.

D) Feeling more anxious at being unemployed than upset or angry at her employers is consistent with a nervous, practical-minded character who is less concerned with matters of justice and injustice, and more concerned with the practical and material aspects of life.

E) Taking the firing philosophically and phlegmatically is consistent with a strong-minded, self-contained character who is perhaps well educated in the classics, or, alternatively, with a defeated, depressed character who adopts a philosophical stance so as to mask and disguise her depression. *After being fired for blowing the whistle, what does your character do?*

Situations to Consider

What would your character do if:

- Someone she knew was about to use the product?
- She had reason to use the product?
- She suspected that others in the office were preparing to blow the whistle?
- She was moved to another department after reporting the flaw to a superior?
- She was ordered to destroy all documents concerning the product?
- After blowing the whistle, she was attacked on all sides?
- After blowing the whistle, she received an award?

Other Whistle-Blowing Situations

Put your character in the most appropriate of the following situations and think through how she would act and react. If you like, flesh out the scene by adding one conflict and one surprise.

- a military massacre
- a political scandal
- a church scandal
- a business scheme to defraud
- cheating on a test
- a date rape
- impropriety of a family member

The Pressure to Conform

Most people do not blow the whistle because they find it safer to conform. A classic experiment in social psychology, conducted by research psychologist Solomon Asch, proved how powerfully people experience the need to conform. Psychology professor C. George Boeree noted in an article titled "Conformity and Obedience" (www.ship.edu/~cgboeree/conformity.html)

that volunteers in the Asch experiment, surrounded by peers who were really confederates of Asch and who gave clearly wrong answers about the length of a line they were shown, felt significant pressure to provide what they themselves must have known were incorrect answers. Boeree explained:

> Even in this rather unthreatening social situation, 35 percent of the time subjects in this experiment gave what were clearly wrong responses.

Not only that: The more times the process is repeated, the more likely it is that you will finally conform. In Asch's studies, only 10 percent of the subjects stuck to their guns to the end. Only one in ten! Ninety percent ultimately conformed. Think through what this suggests about the character you're investigating. Is she one of the rare ones or quite average when it comes to nonconformity?

Did You Know?

People conform less and are more likely to blow the whistle if even one person agrees with their assessment of the situation. Conversely, when the group is unanimous in its opinion, even if that opinion is obviously wrong, it proves profoundly hard for a lone individual to disagree. Boeree explained:

> Group unanimity is perhaps the strongest variable in Asch's research. In the original studies, the stooges were always in unanimous agreement. All you need is one stooge not to conform and the spell is broken. This is true even when the non-conforming stooge is still giving a wrong answer!

Food for Thought

• What qualities of character are required for a person to blow the whistle? Does your character possess those qualities?

• What set of circumstances would make it more likely for your character to blow the whistle, and what set of circumstances would make it less likely?

• Is some other character in your novel a natural whistle-blower? Which character is it?

SCENARIO NO. 11

POKER NIGHT

Imagine that your character is taking part in an intense, high-stakes poker game. There is a lot of money to be made and a lot of money to be lost, the other players are veteran poker players, and the action is nonstop. Picture the other players at the table: Invent an interesting mix of male and female gamblers, some from Europe and Southeast Asia, one in a ten-gallon hat, another in a loud Hawaiian shirt, another looking like a corporate attorney. Set the scene in detail and get in the spirit of high-stakes poker.

Picture your character sitting down at the table. Get into his skin. Feel the poker chips, the cloth of the table, the cards as they're dealt. Enjoy the action—and address the following questions.

1. What sort of poker player would your character make?

   A) Cautious?
   B) Impulsive?
   C) Friendly while ahead, gloomy when losing?
   D) Poker-faced and cool?
   E) Flamboyant?

A) Playing cautiously is consistent with a character who is cautious in other aspects of his life, someone who likes to reduce or eliminate risks whenever possible, prefers not losing to winning, and experiences real anxiety whenever he makes a big bet or takes a big risk.

B) Playing impulsively is consistent with an impulsive character who may manage his impulsive nature through efforts at strict control, for instance, by controlling his body weight through rigorous exercise or starvation, and who is likely the one leaving the card room on a motorcycle—after a few too many drinks.

C) Acting friendly when ahead and gloomy when losing is consistent with a conventional character whose moods are dependent on immediate circumstances and who will be easy to read at the table, as good hands will involuntarily excite him and bad hands will show his frustration and annoyance.

D) Maintaining a poker face and playing coolly is consistent with a calculating character who knows pot odds, mixes up his game by sometimes playing conservatively and sometimes bluffing, and is probably successful at business.

E) Playing flamboyantly is consistent with an immature character who is defensively posturing so as to mask his underling anxiety, or, alternatively, with a savvy character who is trying to throw other players off their game—or, quite possibly, with both.

What sort of poker player would your character make?

2. After winning a big pot, would your character?

    A) Modestly say, "Good hand"?
    B) Gloat?
    C) Wear a deadpan expression?
    D) Apologize?
    E) Exclaim, "It's about time!"?

A) Modestly saying "Good hand," is consistent with an even-tempered character who empathizes with others and is likely one-half of a long-term, enduring intimate relationship.

B) Gloating is consistent with an immature, oppositional, and perhaps anti-social character who lacks empathy, blames others for his failures, and always has an excuse for losing.

C) Wearing a deadpan expression is consistent with a controlled, calculating character who may be using his deadpan expression to mask feelings of superiority that, if allowed out, would percolate up as gloating.

D) Apologizing is consistent with a socialized character with relatively low self-esteem who is used to playing second fiddle in life or, alternatively, with a crafty character who uses apologizing as one of his tricks at the poker table.

E) Exclaiming "It's about time!" is consistent with a character who believes the world owes him special consideration and who is likely a little on the grandiose and narcissistic side.

What does your character do after winning a big pot?

3. After losing a big pot, would your character?

    A) Fume?
    B) Congratulate the other player?
    C) Hang his head?
    D) Glower?
    E) Act indifferent?

A) Fuming is consistent with a self-centered, probably volatile character who is hard to deal with, hard to live with, and hard to like.

B) Congratulating the other player is consistent with an even-tempered character who reacts philosophically to life's defeats or, alternatively, with a character who uses the mild irony of congratulation to mask his true feelings of irritation and upset.

C) Hanging his head is consistent with a character who lacks resilience, bounces back poorly from defeats, and likely has not met many of his goals in life.

D) Glowering is consistent with a self-absorbed character who is likely demanding, defensive, poor at relationships, and possibly emotionally and physically abusive.

E) Acting indifferently is consistent with a philosophical, phlegmatic character whose self-image is not harmed by losing, with a bored character who is too depressed to care about winning or losing, or with a practiced character good at wearing a mask of indifference to hide his true feelings.

What does your character do after losing a big pot?

4. Another player is needling your character, saying things like "I've got your number!" and "You're dead money!" How does your character react?

   A) Pays little or no attention?
   B) Looks indifferent, but fumes inside?
   C) Gives as good as he gets?
   D) Laughs it off?
   E) Pals up to the other players?

A) Paying little or no attention is consistent with a mature character who understands that needling is customary at card games or, alternatively, with a tough-minded, calculating character who is making note of the insult, biding his time, and preparing to get even.

B) Looking indifferent but fuming inside is consistent with a character who feels compelled to fit in but who, because he is swallowing his real feelings, ends up with somatic complaints that require the likes of aspirin and Maalox.

C) Giving as good as he gets is consistent with a self-confident character not inclined to take insults or, alternatively, with a character who grew up in an environment where, if you didn't respond instantly to threat, you got steam-rolled—say, for instance, as one of five or six aggressive siblings.

D) Laughing it off is consistent with a secure, self-confident character who is rarely buffeted by the words and actions of others and who knows how to take his own counsel in the face of criticism and insults.

E) Palling up to the other players is consistent with a crafty character good at forming strategic alliances and probably successful at business or, alternatively, with a character lacking in self-confidence who seeks out group support to make up for individual inadequacy.

How does your character react to needling?

• **卫** •

5. Your character has lost more money than he had intended to lose. What does your character do when he gets home?

    A) Quietly explain the situation?
    B) Loudly announce his losses and break some dishes?
    C) Beg for forgiveness and pledge never to gamble again?
    D) Demand more money so that he can get even?
    E) Act morose and out-of-sorts but remain tight-lipped about the losses?

• •

A) Quietly explaining the situation is consistent with a mature, self-confident character who feels emotionally equal to telling the truth, even when the truth is embarrassing and unflattering.

B) Loudly announcing the losses and then breaking some dishes is consistent with a volatile character with poor impulse control who likes to bully people, make scenes, and let other people clean up his messes.

C) Begging for forgiveness and pledging never to gamble again is consistent with a sentimental, maudlin character with addictive tendencies who lives life in cycles, erratic behavior followed by pleas for forgiveness followed by periods of quiet followed by a buildup of tension leading to more impulsive behavior.

D) Demanding more money so as to get even is consistent with a self-centered character who tramples over other people, blames the world for his problems, and is always digging new holes out of which he never really escapes.

E) Acting morose but remaining tight-lipped about the losses is consistent with a self-contained character who prefers not to share much of his inner life with others and who is likely emotionally unavailable for other people.

After losing a lot of money, what does your character do when he gets home?

• **卫** •

6. What does your character like about poker?

    A) Winning money?

B) Beating other players?
c) Socializing?
D) Mastering the game?
E) Feeling excited?

. . . .

A) Liking to win money is consistent with a materialistic character who is fixated on material aspects of life like bargains, luxury items, hot trends, quick returns, what people earn, and what things cost.

B) Liking to beat other players is consistent with a competitive character who is competitive in all walks of life, from racquetball games at the gym to his child's Saturday soccer games to winning at business—possibly at all costs.

c) Liking to socialize is consistent with a personable, sociable, conventional character with lots of friends and acquaintances who has people-related things planned for every night of the week and all day Saturday and Sunday.

D) Liking to master the game is consistent with a literal-minded character who studies the subjects that interest him and who likes to know the odds in life as well as at the poker table—the odds, for instance, of his new car breaking down or rain ruining his vacation plans.

E) Liking the excitement is consistent with an adrenaline junkie who switches jobs regularly, is constantly on the lookout for new risks to take and new adventures to begin, and finds monogamy boring.

What, if anything, does your character like about poker?

Situations to Consider

What would your character do if:

- He caught another player cheating?
- He began to get a little tipsy?
- He was keeping someone waiting?
- He lost a big pot to a bluff?
- He won a big pot on a bluff?
- He was the only man at the table?
- It came down to a heads-up competition with a friend?

Other Competitive Situations

Put your character in the most appropriate of the following situations and think through how he would act and react. If you like, flesh out the scene by adding one conflict and one surprise.

- chess match
- tug-of-war at a company picnic
- television game show
- pick-up basketball game
- sales competition
- open seating at a rock concert
- competition for an academic prize

At the Casino

Is your character a poker player? Is there some other casino game that fits your character's personality better? Gambling expert Henry Tamburin explained in *Casino Player* magazine (www.casinoplayer.com) that different personality types are drawn to different games:

- If you are outgoing, highly expressive, talk more than you listen, are dominating in conversation and an extrovert, then your game is craps.

- If you are reserved, private, self-aware, listen more than you talk, and an introvert, then your games are slots, video poker, roulette, and mini-baccarat.

- If you are basically a risk-taker, your games are progressive slots, prop bets in craps, jackpot bets in Caribbean stud poker and keno.

- If you are warm, understanding, sensitive, prefer harmony over controversy and find that some people take advantage of you, your games are slots and video poker.

To what casino game is your character drawn? What does that reveal about his personality?

Did You Know?

According to Tamburin, left-brainers do well with games like blackjack, video poker, and table poker, games that require analytical and quantitative thinking, while right-brainers like to play the slot machines.

Food for Thought

• On a scale of 1 to 10, 10 being the most competitive, how competitive is your character?

• Under what circumstances would your character compete unfairly?

• In what circumstances would your character be at his most competitive? In what circumstances would he be least competitive?

SCENARIO NO. 12

ON STAGE

When your character speaks in public, she displays parts of her personality that she otherwise rarely shows. Speaking in public is a performance that, however well rehearsed and carefully managed, nevertheless reveals important information about your character's sense of self, anxiety level, beliefs and opinions, and presence. You may know your character very well within the context of your novel but have little idea how she may comport herself in front of five hundred people—until you put her in that situation in your mind's eye.

Give your character a reason to speak to a large group, imagine her preparing (or not preparing) her speech, picture the day approaching, and then put her on stage in front of several hundred people. Flesh out the venue, the audience, the microphone (is it a podium mike, a lapel mike, a hand mike, a hanging mike?), and the other details of the scene. Get her up on her feet and speaking—what do you notice?

1. How has your character approached preparing? Has she:

   A) Prepared carefully and rehearsed often?
   B) Prepared some and procrastinated some?
   C) Prepared feverishly at the last moment?

D) Meant to prepare but never got around to it?

E) Decided to wing it?

A) Preparing carefully and rehearsing often is consistent with a meticulous, disciplined character or, alternatively, with a highly anxious character who manages her anxiety by trying to gain control and mastery of situations.

B) Preparing some and procrastinating some is a typical reaction and consistent with a character who takes her responsibilities seriously enough but who is neither so anxious nor so disciplined as to prepare and rehearse religiously.

C) Preparing feverishly at the last moment is consistent with an immature character who feels unequal to the challenges of the world and who finds her primary motivation in fear, waiting until the fear is unbearable before taking necessary action.

D) Meaning to prepare but never getting around to it is consistent with a careless, unproductive, possibly spoiled character unlikely to accept that actions have consequences or, alternatively, with a grandiose character who engages in magical thinking and believes that all will be well whether or not she prepares.

E) Deciding to wing it is consistent with a narcissistic character who regularly overrates her abilities and downplays the consequences of her actions or, alternatively, with a highly anxious character who has experienced too much anxiety to prepare and now is likely to freeze and do a wretched job ad-libbing.

How has your character approached preparing?

2. On the day of the speech, what does your character do?

A) Pace nervously and find time moving slowly?

B) Go over her speech several times?

C) Spend a normal day and not think much about the evening's presentation?

D) Self-medicate with a few cocktails?

E) Rush around doing last-minute things and arrive a little late?

A) Pacing nervously and finding the time moving slowly is consistent with an introspective character who likely broods about matters, is troubled by anxieties and negative self-talk, and may be ruled by the dark side of her personality.

B) Going over her speech several times is consistent with a nervous character who handles anxiety by preparing and gaining mastery or, alternatively, with an accomplished character who has learned that practice makes perfect.

C) Spending a normal day and not thinking much about the presentation is consistent with a self-contained, well-adjusted character who can compartmentalize the tasks in her life or, alternatively, with an immature character who is avoiding readying herself for her presentation by keeping to her usual routine.

D) Self-medicating with a few cocktails is consistent with an addictive, anxious character who may succeed in business and in life for a period of time but who is nevertheless on a slippery slope toward full-fledged alcoholism and the unraveling of her life.

E) Rushing around doing last-minute things and arriving a little late is consistent with a character whose primary defense is denial and who, by denying the need to prioritize the speech and to engage in calming activities, sets herself up for a poor presentation made worse by it not beginning on time.

What does your character do on the day of the speech?

3. How comfortable is your character on stage?

    A) Very uncomfortable, and shows it?
    B) Moderately uncomfortable, and shows it?
    c) Moderately uncomfortable, and doesn't show it?
    D) Comfortable enough, so long as things go well?
    E) Extremely comfortable?

A) Feeling very uncomfortable and showing that discomfort is consistent with a character who suffers from full-blown stage fright, whose anxieties, fears, worries, doubts, and phobias play a significant negative role in life, and who is likely anxious—and even phobic—in a variety of other situations and circumstances.

B) Feeling moderately uncomfortable and showing it is consistent with a character who isn't practiced in reducing her anxiety level and who perhaps hasn't had enough experience with presentations to learn how to appear calm, contained, and present even when she is experiencing a few butterflies.

C) Feeling moderately uncomfortable and managing not to show it is consistent with a character who has learned how to mask her feelings and who is likely accomplished in business and easy in social situations, even if such situations provoke some measure of anxiety in her.

D) Feeling comfortable enough, as long as things go well, is consistent with a character who is less self-confident than she appears and who is likely to unexpectedly stumble in situations that take a turn for the worse or that test her self-image.

E) Feeling extremely comfortable is consistent with a self-confident character who is experienced at presenting herself in public or, alternatively, with a grandiose, narcissistic character indifferent to her own poor performances who presumes that she is entitled to applause no matter what.

How comfortable is your character on stage?

4. Does your character:

    A) Read a prepared text without looking up much?
    B) Read a prepared text but make good audience contact?
    C) Speak stiffly from notes?
    D) Speak fluently from notes?
    E) Speak without notes or other props?

A) Reading a prepared text without looking up much is consistent with a closed, stiff character who has difficulty relating in the world, lacks empathy, and is likely narrowly focused on her needs and concerns to the exclusion of other people and the affairs of the world.

B) Reading a prepared text but making good audience contact is consistent with a careful character who knows how to engage with others but who isn't sufficiently practiced or confident to proceed extemporaneously or just from notes.

c) Speaking stiffly from notes is consistent with a character who understands conventional presentation skills and knows she shouldn't just read a speech, but who is nevertheless too anxious and perhaps too unprepared to engage with her audience and speak effectively.

D) Speaking fluently from notes is consistent with a self-confident, accomplished character who is likely to be able to present herself and her ideas well in other settings, whether business or social, and who is also likely a leader in her field.

E) Speaking without notes or other props is consistent with a supremely self-confident character, with a practiced character who has presented this material so often that it is second nature, or with a grandiose character who doesn't deign to prepare and is unconcerned about how her performance is received.

How does your character proceed to give her talk?

5. What best describes your character's public speaking style?

    A) Stiff and heavy-handed?
    B) Anxious?
    c) Ingratiating?
    D) Self-aggrandizing?
    E) Confident?

A) A stiff, heavy-handed style is consistent with a character who is self-conscious and self-involved and likely unused to presenting herself in public situations.

B) An anxious style is consistent with a fearful character who is plagued by negative self-talk, envisions and expects failure, and likely succumbs to regular bouts of stress-induced illness.

c) An ingratiating style is consistent with a sly, possibly promiscuous character who may be the victim of sexual abuse and who uses flirtation and ingratiating ways to deal with and manipulate other people.

D) A self-aggrandizing style is consistent with a character who looks out for herself, enjoys material things and making money, and is likely successful—and perhaps ruthless—in business.

E) A confident style is consistent with a character who is comfortable in her own skin and is likely successful in the world or, alternatively, with a grandiose character who exudes confidence irrespective of her actual accomplishments, skills, or qualities of character.

What best describes your character's speaking style?

6. What does your character do once the speech is finished?

   A) Chat comfortably with audience members?
   B) Chat reluctantly with audience members?
   c) Hide out in a back room?
   D) Feel physically drained and mentally unwell?
   E) Go out for a drink with anybody near at hand?

A) Chatting comfortably with audience members is consistent with a self-confident, empathic character who knows her material, possesses social ease and social graces, and prefers to give more rather than less of herself to others.

B) Chatting reluctantly with audience members is consistent with a stiff character who lacks some self-confidence but who nevertheless feels compelled to chat as part of the requirements of performing and who might be expected to fulfill at least the minimal requirements of any work she undertook.

c) Hiding out in a back room is consistent with a fearful, reclusive character who is unused to performing, has difficulty with strangers and in social situations, and likely lives an isolated, secluded life.

D) Feeling physically drained and mentally unwell is consistent with a character who meets her responsibilities but who is also worn out by them, possibly to such an extent that she burns out and experiences periodic crises and breakdowns.

E) Going out for a drink with anybody near at hand is consistent with a character who manages anxiety and the adrenaline rush that follows performing by socializing and who likely is often embroiled in affairs and interpersonal dramas, usually accompanied by alcohol.

What does your character do once her speech is finished?

Situations to Consider

What would your character do if:

- The microphone failed?
- She forgot what to say?
- The audience was much smaller than anticipated?
- The audience was much larger than anticipated?
- While she was speaking, several people got up and left?
- After the speech, someone asked a question that your character couldn't answer?
- After the speech, an audience member invited your character out for a drink?

Other Performance Situations

Put your character in the most appropriate of the following situations and think through how she would act and react. If you like, flesh out the scene by adding one conflict and one surprise.

- main toast at a wedding
- important presentation at work
- eulogy at a funeral service
- testimony before a congressional committee
- presentation at a professional conference
- sales presentation to new clients
- amateur choral performance at a holiday concert

The Experience of Performance Anxiety

If you want to paint a realistic picture of a character suffering from performance anxiety, what sorts of symptoms would you employ? Here's a symptom picture scale compiled by Marilyn Gellis and Rosemary Muat in their book *The Twelve Steps of Phobics Anonymous*. It includes symptoms associated with mild, moderate, and severe bouts of stage fright, rated on a scale of 1 to 10.

FUNCTIONAL

1. Butterflies, a queasy feeling in the stomach; trembling; jitteriness; tension.
2. Clammy palms; hot flashes and all-over warmth; profuse sweating.
3. Very rapid, strong, racing, pounding, or irregular heartbeat; tremors; muscle tension and aches; fatigue.

DECREASED FUNCTIONAL ABILITY

4. Jelly legs; weakness in the knees; wobbly, unsteady feelings; shakiness.
5. Immediate desperate and urgent need to escape, avoid, or hide.
6. A lump in the throat; dry mouth; choking; muscle tension.
7. Hyperventilation; tightness in chest; shortness of breath; smothering sensation.

VERY LIMITED OR COMPLETELY NONFUNCTIONAL

8. Feelings of impending doom or death; high pulse rate; difficulty breathing; palpitations.
9. Dizziness; visual distortion; faintness; headache; nausea; numbness; tingling of hands, feet, or other body parts; diarrhea; frequent urination.

COMPLETE PANIC

10. Nonfunctional; disorientation; detachment; feelings of unreality; paralysis; fear of dying, going crazy, or losing control. (Frequently people experiencing their first spontaneous panic attack rush to emergency rooms convinced that they are having a heart attack.)

When you consider how your character will react to getting up on stage to deliver an important speech, also consider how her anxiety will manifest itself.

Did You Know?

Public speaking is one common phobia—the most common. But there are literally hundreds of phobias. There is almost nothing that someone can't fear! Here are some of the "A" phobias listed on Hypnoticworld.com:

ABLUTOPHOBIA: fear of washing or bathing

ACEROPHOBIA: fear of sourness

ACOUSTICOPHOBIA: fear of noise

AEROPHOBIA: fear of drafts

AGATEOPHOBIA: fear of insanity

AGRIZOOPHOBIA: fear of wild animals

AGYROPHOBIA: fear of crossing the street

ALBUMINUROPHOBIA: fear of kidney disease

ALEKTOROPHOBIA: fear of chickens

ALLIUMPHOBIA: fear of garlic

ALLODOXAPHOBIA: fear of opinions

AMATHOPHOBIA: fear of dust

AMAXOPHOBIA: fear of riding in a car

AMEROPHOBIA: fear of American culture

ANTHROPHOBIA: fear of flowers

ANTLOPHOBIA: fear of floods

APEIROPHOBIA: fear of infinity

APOTEMNOPHOBIA: fear of persons with amputations

ARACHIBUTYROPHOBIA: fear of peanut butter sticking to the roof of the mouth

AULOPHOBIA: fear of flutes

Given what you know about your character, which of her fears, if any, rise to the level of phobia?

Food for Thought

• Imagine your character giving her first large presentation. Imagine her giving her fiftieth. What differences do you detect?

• Ten being the highest and one being the lowest, how much public-speaking charisma does your character possess?

• If it seems to you that your character would be made anxious by having to give a speech before five hundred people, can you identify what about the experience would make her most anxious?

SCENARIO NO. 13
VIVID DREAM

What does your character dream about? How you answer depends a lot on what you think dreams represent. If you believe they are relatively random pastiches of the day's events with little significance, then you'll conceptualize your character's dreams one way. If you think they are meaningful, dynamic metaphors for inner conflicts, worries, and other pressing issues, you will conceptualize them another way. Consider both your understanding of what dreams represent and what you imagine this character would dream about, and picture one of your character's typical vivid dreams.

Picture this vivid dream as if you were sitting in a movie theater watching it. How does it begin? Who are the actors? What are the dynamic issues at play? What does it reveal about your character's personality? Enjoy the dream as you would enjoy a good movie, accompany the viewing with some popcorn, and consider what you've learned.

1. Is the dream primarily:

A) An anxiety dream, for instance, with your character being chased or falling?

B) A sex dream?

C) An adventure dream?

D) A dream about a recognizable upcoming challenge?

E) A dream about some traumatic event in the past?

A) A vivid anxiety dream is consistent with a character who is under considerable general stress that has been punctuated by a new, provocative source of stress, producing an anxiety overload.

B) A vivid sex dream is consistent with a meek character who may sublimate her sex drive into the realm of fantasy, or, alternatively, with a robust character with healthy appetites whose lustiness may have gotten activated by a recent encounter with someone attractive and appealing.

C) A vivid adventure dream is consistent with a character who may be bored and hungry for an exciting change, at least at the level of vicarious fantasy.

D) A vivid dream about a recognizable upcoming challenge is consistent with a responsible character who broods about her duties and works on ways of responding to challenges as she sleeps.

E) A vivid dream about some past traumatic event is consistent with a character who may be suffering from post-traumatic stress disorder or who, at the very least, is sufficiently burdened by the past that it is intruding into and influencing the present.

What is your character's vivid dream primarily about?

2. If this is a recurrent dream, what appears to be its source?

A) Stress?

B) Depression?

C) Fear?

D) Obsession?

E) Uncertainty?

A) If the dream recurs because of stress, that is consistent with a character significantly burdened by her worries who carries those worries into the night and who is likely cautious, brooding, and self-absorbed during her waking hours.

B) If the dream recurs because of depression, that is consistent with a chronically depressed character who is likely to suffer from insomnia and low energy levels and is unlikely to find pleasure in her pursuits.

C) If the dream recurs because of fear, that is consistent with a timid character who organizes her life around self-protection, from extra locks on the doors to hiding from view even when in the company of others.

D) If the dream recurs because of obsession, that is consistent with an avid, compulsive character with an addictive nature who organizes her life around her obsessions and addictions.

E) If the dream recurs because of uncertainty, that is consistent with a confused, indecisive character who keeps her life on hold because of the anxiety that wells up in her when she's confronted by any choice, even of the most trivial sort.

Why does your character's vivid dream tend to recur?

3. Under what circumstances would your character write down the dream?

    A) If it seemed revealing?
    B) If it seemed especially vivid?
    C) If it seemed like an omen?
    D) If it involved a particular person?
    E) Never?

A) Writing down the dream when the dream seems revealing is consistent with a thoughtful, self-aware person on the lookout for opportunities to better understand herself and actively learn from herself.

B) Writing down the dream when the dream seems especially vivid is consistent with a character who readily responds to sense data and might, because of her sensitivity, find herself overwhelmed in situations with lots of sensory stimulation, like crowded department stores or loud parties.

c) Writing down the dream if the dream seems like an omen is consistent with a superstitious character who is likely a fan of numerology, astrology, New Age metaphysics, and tales of the supernatural.

D) Writing down the dream if it involves a particular person is consistent with a character with a keen interest in interpersonal dynamics and relationships who is likely to prize drama and romance.

E) Never writing down any of her dreams is consistent with a matter-of-fact character who doubts that dreams are anything more than the trivial, meaningless firings of her brain.

Under what circumstances would your character write down her vivid dream?

4. Does your character see her dreams as:

    A) Fascinating but insignificant?
    B) Fascinating and significant?
    C) Troubling and unwanted?
    D) The literal truth?
    E) Meaningless and overrated?

A) Viewing dreams as fascinating but insignificant is consistent with a character at once creative and scientific, someone who values art and imagination but is skeptical about the claims for the meaningfulness of dreams unless those claims can be tested by the scientific method.

B) Viewing dreams as fascinating and significant is consistent with a character who credits herself with a soulful, spiritual nature, who likely belongs to an organized religion, and who feels drawn to mythological fables and tales.

C) Viewing dreams as troubling and unwanted is consistent with a tormented character who is burdened by her inner life and by the dynamic, unresolved conflicts that cause her stress and pain.

D) Viewing dreams as the literal truth is consistent with a naïve character with conventional beliefs and opinions who is likely to engage in little self-analysis and who prefers received wisdom to self-awareness.

E) Viewing dreams as meaningless and overrated is consistent with a skeptical, perhaps cynical and ironic character who is likely troubled by recurrent meaning crises and an enduring, low-grade depression.

How does your character view her dreams?

5. To whom would your character tell this dream?

    A) Mate?
    B) Therapist?
    C) Best friend?
    D) Parent?
    E) To no one?

A) Telling the dream to her mate is consistent with a character in a close, intimate, and, perhaps, enmeshed relationship where partners confide in each other and may also burden each other with unnecessary details of their inner lives.

B) Telling the dream to her therapist is consistent with an intelligent, troubled, and perhaps dependent character, probably of the professional or artistic class, who seeks guidance and support from others and may have trouble with independent action.

C) Telling the dream to her best friend is consistent with a character who enjoys the company of her friends and who tries to nurture relationships over time and distance.

D) Telling the dream to her parents is consistent with a youthful character who views her parents as confidantes, with an open character who has an unusually intimate and stress-free relationship with her parents, or, alternatively, with a dependent, enmeshed character who maintains unhealthy ties with her parents.

E) Refusing to tell the dream to anyone is consistent with a closed, reclusive, probably unsympathetic character or, alternatively, with a strong, private character used to relying on her own guidance and her own devices.

In whom would your character confide her dream?

6. Your character is given a gift of a free session with a dream analyst. Does she treat the analysis as:

A) Gospel?
B) Suggestive and interesting?
C) Personally upsetting?
D) Creative but unreliable?
E) Hogwash?

A) Treating dream analysis as gospel is consistent with a naïve character who believes uncritically in the putative expertise of self-styled experts and who likely has trouble taking fully independent action.

B) Treating dream analysis as suggestive and interesting is consistent with an artistic character who has likely written, painted, or played a musical instrument, and who keeps or has kept dream journals.

C) Treating dream analysis as personally upsetting is consistent with an anxious, superstitious character who organizes her life around the warnings to be found in fortune cookies and astrology columns.

D) Treating dream analysis as creative but unreliable is consistent with a character who is forthright and independent-minded, and equally at home creating and thinking critically.

E) Treating dream analysis as hogwash is consistent with a skeptical character who is likely more interested in disproving putative experts than following them and probably prizes independent thinking and autonomous action above all other qualities.

How does your character treat dream analysis?

Situations to Consider

What would your character do if:

- She was plagued by a recurring nightmare?
- Someone asked your character for a dream interpretation?
- She was awakened in the middle of the night by a vivid dream and couldn't get back to sleep?

- She felt strongly that the dream portended a disaster?
- She suddenly stopped dreaming?
- She suddenly started dreaming?
- She received as a gift a book of dream interpretations?

Other Dream-Like Situations

Put your character in the most appropriate of the following situations and think through how she would act and react. If you like, flesh out the scene by adding one conflict and one surprise.

- hallucinogenic drug trip
- desert mirage
- vision quest
- long stretch without sleep
- coming out of anesthesia
- near-death experience
- disorienting psychological experiment

Nightmare Disorder

A nightmare is a dream that usually occurs in the latter part of the night and that elicits strong feelings of inescapable fear. Most nightmares are a normal reaction to stress and may be one of the primary ways human beings work through traumatic events. Nightmares like falling, being chased, or being attacked begin in childhood and tend to be more common in girls than in boys. Imagine your character experiences the occasional nightmare. What might its content be? Why that content?

Does your character suffer from recurrent nightmares? If those recurrent nightmares start to impair social, occupational, or other important areas of functioning, they lead to the diagnosis of Nightmare Disorder (formerly Dream Anxiety Disorder). Nightmares run the gamut from perfectly normal and no particular problem to a serious disorder that can wreak havoc with sleep patterns and psychological health. As you investigate your character's personality, ask yourself the question, "What nightmares are likely with a personality of this type?"

Did You Know?

According to *Psychology Today* (www.psychologytoday.com), the following are some common causes of nightmares:

- anxiety or stress (the most common cause; a major life event precedes the onset of nightmares in 60 percent of cases)
- illness with a fever
- death of a loved one (bereavement)
- adverse reaction to or side effect of a drug
- recent withdrawal from a drug such as sleeping pills
- effect of alcohol or excessive alcohol consumption
- abrupt alcohol withdrawal
- breathing disorder in sleep (sleep apnea)
- sleep disorders (narcolepsy, sleep terror disorder)
- an inherited tendency toward nightmares

If your character is a heavy drinker, has lost a loved one, is down with a high fever, or is getting off drugs, a nightmare may be in order.

Food for Thought

- Is your character someone who finds her dreams important or unimportant?
- Might a dream figure in your current novel?
- Have you had a vivid dream that might make for a novel?

SCENARIO NO. 14

A BORING DAY

Your character is suffering through an excruciatingly boring day. A day like this can be very revealing because it may be the first time in a long time that your character stops to reflect on his current circumstances and path in life. To suddenly find yourself significantly bored is an existential crisis that has led people to throw over their job for a new pursuit, bolt from a relationship, or commit suicide. Take the opportunity of this scenario to think through how your character will react when confronted by intense boredom.

First, set up the boring day. Maybe it's a rainy Sunday and a power outage prevents his usual routine of watching a full day of sports on television. Maybe it's a day when a series of meetings have been canceled and your character doesn't know what to do with himself. Maybe it's a dull day on a business trip. Or maybe it's an ordinary day, just like every other day, whose ordinariness suddenly seems unbearable. Get a clear picture of your character, his life, and how a boring day might suddenly arise to envelop him.

1. Is your character:

    A) Bored most of the time?
    B) Frequently bored?

c) Sometimes bored?

D) Rarely bored?

E) Never bored?

. . . .

A) Being bored most of the time is consistent with an intelligent, educated, modern character suffering from depression or, alternatively, with a constitutionally gloomy, negative, critical character without interests or enthusiasms.

B) Frequently being bored is consistent with a character who cycles between enthusiasms and depression, perhaps because of a clinical bipolar disorder or perhaps because the work he does is too mechanical and unrewarding.

c) Sometimes being bored is consistent with a character who has carved out a reasonably satisfying life but who is nevertheless intelligent enough, troubled enough, or susceptible enough to meaning crises to sometimes feel the meaning leak out of his pursuits and activities.

D) Rarely being bored is consistent with a well-adjusted, optimistic character who has learned how to keep himself busy, has hobbies and interests that adequately fill up spare time, and doesn't spend too much time brooding about the meaning of life or the workings of the cosmos.

E) Never being bored is consistent with a happy, busy character or, alternatively, with a dull, conventional character pulled along by society's devices who fits in, blends in, and is boring rather than bored.

How often is your character bored?

. . . .  . . . .

2. What is likely to precipitate your character's boredom?

A) His job?

B) His relationships?

c) A lack of compelling interests?

D) Unfulfilled dreams?

E) General depression?

. . . .

A) Having boredom precipitated by his job is consistent with a character who has chosen work with his head and not his heart and is now stuck doing work that doesn't engage or motivate him or, alternatively, with a character who was forced by circumstance into a line of work, like a family business or class-determined occupation, that he is too smart for or that simply doesn't hold his interest.

B) Having boredom precipitated by his relationships is consistent with an intelligent, introspective character who prefers solitude and his own devices to relationships or, alternatively, with a character who enters into relationships for strategic or culture-based reasons and who is then bored, and likely irritated, with the results.

C) Having boredom precipitated by a lack of compelling interests is consistent with an intelligent, educated person who has "seen through" life's pursuits and doesn't find any of them intrinsically meaningful or, alternatively, with a dull, privileged character who is jaded and surfeited by the activities and baubles of his class and position.

D) Having boredom precipitated by unfulfilled dreams is consistent with a sensitive, romantic, dreamy character whose hopes and aspirations—to dance, to sing, to paint, to travel, to make a difference—have been thwarted and dashed, and who is left marking time through life while mourning what might have been.

E) Having boredom precipitated by general depression is consistent with a pessimistic, troubled, gloomy character who is constitutionally under the weather, critical and negative, and possibly suicidal.

What is likely to precipitate your character's boredom?

3. What does your character typically do when bored?

A) Self-medicate?
B) Get busy?
C) Generate false enthusiasm?
D) Brood?
E) Sink into paralysis and depression?

A) Self-medicating when bored is consistent with a depressed, addictive character who uses chemicals to change and improve his mood and who will likely begin organizing his life around using substances, the very interest he takes in securing and using those drugs becoming the primary way he relieves his boredom.

B) Getting busy when bored is consistent with a disciplined, self-aware character who knows intuitively or has learned through experience that activity is the best antidote to boredom and the surest way to quiet a brooding, self-absorbed mind.

C) Generating false enthusiasm when bored is consistent with a defensive, conventional character who has learned to put on a happy face when bored and throw himself into pursuits that hold no particular meaning but that are socially acceptable and easy to defend.

D) Brooding when bored is consistent with an intelligent, educated character who relishes his solitude, is reclusive by nature, and likely spends a lot of time chewing on—but not being able to answer—life's large questions.

E) Sinking into paralysis and depression when bored is consistent with a disturbed character filled with serious inner conflicts who likely has a history of trauma and episodes of major depression.

What does your character typically do when bored?

4. What sort of crisis might your character precipitate out of boredom?

    A) Drive fast and have a wreck?
    B) Try a new, dangerous drug?
    C) Get embroiled in an interpersonal intrigue?
    D) Have an unwise affair?
    E) Shoplift?

A) Driving fast and having a wreck is consistent with a high-energy character whose problem has to do with finding activities engaging enough—and physical enough—to allow for the channeling of overflowing adrenaline and abundant energy.

b) Trying a new, dangerous drug is consistent with a character with low self-esteem and impulse control problems who is self-destructive, careless in life, and a risk both to himself and to others.

c) Getting embroiled in an interpersonal intrigue is consistent with a character whose primary method of changing his mood is via social interactions and who is likely to have a large number of acquaintances, a great many hobbies and pursuits, and a history of party-hopping and clique-joining.

d) Having an unwise affair is consistent with a character who turns to love and sex to alleviate boredom, likely has trouble maintaining monogamous relationships, and has a colorful past littered with dramatic (and traumatic) marriages and liaisons.

e) Shoplifting is consistent with a character who relieves boredom by engaging in dangerous, self-destructive behaviors and who is likely to have an addictive personality, tempestuous relationships, and a penchant for sudden, risky adventures.

What sort of crisis might your character precipitate out of boredom?

5. What might help relieve your character's boredom?

    A) A call from a good friend?
    B) Going out to see a foreign movie?
    C) A conscious decision to switch moods?
    D) Returning to his creative work?
    E) A weekend out of town?

A) If receiving a call from a good friend is able to relieve your character's boredom, that is consistent with a character for whom boredom is a relatively minor problem and who finds that simple activities like hobbies and friendships will keep him on an even keel.

B) If going to see a foreign movie is able to relieve your character's boredom, that is consistent with an intelligent, romantic character who may be primarily bored with his culture and is likely to pine for other places and maybe even uproot himself one day to live in some exotic locale.

c) If a conscious decision to switch moods is able to relieve your character's boredom, that is consistent with a self-aware character who may employ Eastern or Western practices like meditation or biofeedback, and who is able to monitor and control his moods by paying attention to them.

d) If returning to his creative work is able to relieve your character's boredom, that is consistent with a character who needs his creative outlets and who will experience depression, and even despair, if he is prevented by circumstance or the shadow side of his personality from expressing his creative nature.

e) If a weekend out of town is able to relieve your character's boredom, that is consistent with a well-adjusted but overworked character who needs a change of pace and change of place to refresh his batteries.

What would help relieve your character's boredom?

6. Does your character consider himself:

    A) Considerably more bored than other people?
    B) Somewhat more bored than other people?
    c) About as bored as other people?
    D) Somewhat less bored than other people?
    E) Considerably less bored than other people?

A) Considering himself considerably more bored than other people is consistent with a character who may feel superior to other people, more burdened with existential awareness than other people, more intelligent than other people, and/or more honest than other people.

B) Considering himself somewhat more bored than other people is consistent with a character who suspects that he suffers from a relatively constant background case of the blues and who recognizes that boredom is a persistent issue that he can manage but never completely solve.

c) Considering himself about as bored as other people is consistent with a character who likes to view himself as average, normal, and just like other people and who falls into step with the pursuits and activities of the people around him.

D) Considering himself somewhat less bored than other people is consistent with a character who believes that he has created sufficient interests and a rich enough life that he can hold boredom at bay most of the time.

E) Considering himself considerably less bored than other people is consistent with a character who prides himself on his resourcefulness, who is likely ambitious and successful at business, and who probably considers other people slackers and malcontents.

What is your character's self-image with respect to boredom?

Situations to Consider

What would your character do if:

- He couldn't rid himself of his intense feelings of boredom?
- A boring afternoon passed into an even more boring evening?
- He realized that boredom is sometimes a symptom of depression?
- He began yawning uncontrollably at work?
- Someone close to your character called him boring?
- The things your character used to love no longer interested him?
- His boredom began to feel overwhelming?

Other Boring Situations

Put your character in the most appropriate of the following situations and think through how he would act and react. If you like, flesh out the scene by adding one conflict and one surprise.

- stranded on a desert island
- sequestered during a trial
- crossing Siberia by train
- engaged in assembly line work
- attending a tedious lecture
- making small talk at a company party
- doing the same job for thirty years

The Intelligent Bored and the Jaded Bored

A character who is highly intelligent may be bored because he experiences conventional life as shallow. A jaded character may be bored because he has it too easy. Thus the physicist and the heir may find themselves bored at the same party, but for very different reasons.

According to the Medicor Lab's The Health Center (www.thehealth center.info):

> Very bright people often take most of the information out of a stimulus before others do and they are ready to move on when others are still interested. They get "saturated" with objects or other persons quickly and become bored with them. Another factor in boredom is the "too much, too soon" phenomenon, where an individual is treated in youth like a prince or a princess. Diana Barrymore, daughter of the famous John Barrymore, wrote an autobiography with the title *Too Much, Too Soon* in which she describes a self-destructive lifestyle arising in part from boredom. The motion picture actor Errol Flynn in his autobiography *My Wicked, Wicked Ways* portrays his life in a similar manner.

Did You Know?

Signs of boredom include:

- frequent drowsiness
- the slow passage of time
- vanity and self-absorption
- listlessness and fatigue
- moderate to severe depression
- lack of commitment to goals and plans
- wishful thinking
- preoccupation with romantic or heroic fantasies
- vague discontent

Food for Thought

- What would it mean if your character never experienced boredom? In what set of circumstances would that be a positive and in what set of circumstances would that be a negative?

- Is your character more bored during one time of the day, the week, or the year than at other times?

- On a scale of 1 to 10, 10 being the most bored, how bored is your character on an average day?

SCENARIO NO. 15

ROAD ADVENTURE

Imagine that your character decides to take off on a road adventure (think *On The Road*, *The Adventures of Huckleberry Finn*, *Thelma & Louise*, or any other road adventure book or movie). If taking off on such an adventure doesn't really fit your character's nature, you will also need to dream up a set of circumstances that might provoke your meek or settled character to suddenly hit the road.

Picture your character's preparations, how much money he takes, what he packs, the kind of car he drives, whether you want a sidekick along on the adventure, and other details that will help make the scene come alive in your mind. Then proceed to the following questions.

1. What is your character leaving behind?

   A) A mate?
   B) A mate and children?
   C) A boring job?
   D) A stressful life?
   E) A crime?

A) Leaving a mate behind is consistent with a weak character who hasn't the courage or the emotional wherewithal to end the relationship properly or, alternatively, a flamboyant character in a turbulent relationship who pops in and out of relationships on a whim.

B) Leaving a mate and children behind is consistent with an immature, irresponsible, and selfish character who is too self-absorbed and narcissistic to act honorably or, alternatively, with a desperate character so worn down by duties and responsibilities that running off feels like the only way out.

C) Leaving a boring job behind is consistent with a meek, mild-mannered character who decides that if he wants some excitement in life it will be on his shoulders to find it.

D) Leaving a stressful life behind is consistent with a Type A character who has succumbed to the tensions of modern life and a pressure-packed job, and who is looking not just for adventure but for simplicity and a break from never-ending work as well.

E) Leaving a crime behind is consistent with a dangerous character on a spree whose definition of adventure is likely to include alcohol, drugs, sex, and more crimes to follow.

What is your character leaving behind?

2. What primary emotion does your character experience as he takes off on his adventure?

    A) Excitement?
    B) Fear?
    C) Anger?
    D) Relief?
    E) Indifference?

A) Experiencing excitement is consistent with a thrill-seeking character who needs an adrenaline rush in order to feel alive or, alternatively, with a character who has lived quietly but who has long dreamed of breaking free and who is now excited at finally realizing his dream.

B) Experiencing fear is consistent with an anxious character who is conflicted about running off on this adventure and who is likely to turn right around when a problem or a danger arises—or even at the first hint of difficulty.

C) Experiencing anger is consistent with a rageful character for whom this road adventure is an opportunity to express road rage or some other antisocial, self-absorbed, criminal-leaning aspect of his personality.

D) Experiencing relief is consistent with a character who has been forced through family upbringing and circumstance to toe the line and who has been pining for a long time, maybe his whole life, to hit the road.

E) Experiencing indifference is consistent with a bored, depressed character who is incapable of experiencing either pleasure or excitement, and who sees this road adventure as neither interesting nor amusing but as something to do to kill more time.

What primary emotion does your character experience as he takes off?

3. Your character spots a hitchhiker who doesn't look threatening. Does your character:

    A) Speed up and pass the hitchhiker?
    B) Slow down but decide against stopping?
    C) Stop, take a closer look, and then decide?
    D) Pick up the hitchhiker and engage pleasantly with her?
    E) Pick up the hitchhiker and engage warily with her?

A) Speeding up and passing the hitchhiker is consistent with a cautious, fearful character who perhaps has experienced serious trauma in his life or who has been taught to believe that all strangers are dangerous.

B) Slowing down but deciding against stopping is consistent with a character who internally debates matters and whose free spirit is often overridden by his sense of caution.

C) Stopping to take a closer look is consistent with a relatively fearless character who would like to befriend others and have adventures, but who is cautious and sensible enough not to suppose that all hitchhikers are safe to befriend.

D) Picking up the hitchhiker and engaging pleasantly with her is consistent with a naïve character who is unaware of the real dangers that exist in the world or, alternatively, with a fearless character who is sure of his powers of self-protection.

E) Picking up the hitchhiker and engaging warily with her is consistent with a compassionate but careful character who is confident enough to stop and help, but not so naïve as to suppose that there is no danger associated with helping strangers.

What does your character do when he spots a hitchhiker?

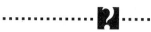

4. Your character is passing through a dry town in Kentucky and is invited to drink with a group of good ol' boys, among them the town sheriff. Does he:

A) Say no nervously and get out of there as quickly as possible?
B) Say no reluctantly?
C) Act noncommittal, so as to get away?
D) Say yes reluctantly?
E) Say yes enthusiastically?

A) Saying no nervously and getting out of there quickly is consistent with a fearful character who prefers safety to adventure or, alternatively, with a character who has had very little experience of the world and is frightened by the newness and strangeness of this experience.

B) Saying no reluctantly is consistent with a character torn between commonsense self-protection and a desire for adventure who in most circumstances, including this one, comes down on the side of safety.

C) Acting noncommittally, so as to get away, is consistent with a savvy, world-wise character who knows that in many situations it is better to temporize and create space for flight than to say yes or no directly.

D) Saying yes reluctantly is consistent with a meek, malleable character who is often drawn into dangerous, unpleasant, or unwanted situations because he hasn't the strength to say no.

E) Saying yes enthusiastically is consistent with a wild-spirited, maybe pre-alcoholic or already alcoholic character who is on this road adventure truly looking for adventure and the opportunity to give free reign to his desires—and maybe his vices and addictions.

How would your character react if invited to drink in a dry county?

5. At a rest stop, your character strikes up a conversation with an attractive stranger who, it turns out, is also on a road adventure. Does your character:

    A) Slip away without saying goodbye?
    B) End the conversation warily and then go on his way?
    c) End the conversation reluctantly and then go on his way?
    D) Invite himself on the attractive stranger's adventure?
    E) Invite the attractive stranger to join him?

A) Slipping away without saying goodbye is consistent with a self-protective, closed, and perhaps repressed character whose modus operandi is to run away from sexual encounters.

B) Ending the conversation warily is consistent with a mildly paranoid character who, even though attracted to this stranger, is more suspicious than attracted and who finds sinister motives in even the most casual and innocent of interactions.

c) Ending the conversation reluctantly is consistent with a shy, cautious, conflicted character who is eager for adventure but whose eagerness is outweighed by shyness and a need for self-protection.

D) Joining the attractive stranger on her adventure is consistent with a bold, fearless, risk-taking character whose life is not organized around conventional routine and who can be expected to crave adventure his entire life.

E) Inviting the attractive stranger to join him is consistent with a strong, self-contained, and self-confident character who presumes that people will fall in with his plans, rather than he falling in with theirs.

How does your character react to meeting an attractive stranger at a rest stop?

6. How does your character's adventure end?

    A) He returns home richer and wiser?
    B) He returns home defeated and deflated?
    c) He arrives somewhere and starts a new life?
    D) He arrives somewhere and repeats his old ways?
    E) He arrives somewhere but only to pause before his next adventure?

A) Returning home richer and wiser is consistent with a strong, solid character who can relish—and learn from—his adventures and misadventures.

B) Returning home defeated and deflated is consistent with an unhappy, negative, self-critical character who has trouble finding pleasure in life and who is so burdened by his personality that escape from it, as for instance, on a road adventure, isn't really possible.

c) Arriving somewhere and starting a new life is consistent with a character with a lot of psychological baggage to shed who, perhaps as a result of embarking on this adventure, has already shed some of that baggage and is primed to shed even more.

D) Arriving somewhere and repeating his old ways is consistent with a character with low self-esteem who lacks self-awareness, is on the run from himself, and will continue to run until he gains insight into his personality and his own self-destructive tendencies.

E) Arriving somewhere but only to pause is consistent with a restless, alienated, and, perhaps, troubled character who feels out of step with settled society and who presumes there is no place where he will ever fit in or call home.

How does your character's road adventure end?

Situations to Consider

What would your character do if:

- He started running out of money?
- He called home and learned that a grandparent was ill?
- He called home and learned that a grandparent had died?

- He was offered a job in a small town?
- He grew lonely on the road?
- He grew tired on the road?
- He grew bored on the road?

Other Adventure Situations

Put your character in the most appropriate of the following situations and think through how he would act and react. If you like, flesh out the scene by adding one conflict and one surprise.

- African safari
- bank robbery
- mountain climbing expedition
- escape from a POW camp
- deep sea treasure hunt
- Las Vegas gambling spree
- bull fighting

Where and What to Risk?

You may want your character to take some risks, so as to create drama in your novel. But where can a contemporary character take real risks? As psychologist Marvin Zuckerman explained in "Are You a Risk Taker," an article published in *Psychology Today* (www.psychologytoday.com):

> Although risk-taking has negative aspects and can even prove fatal, it is a positive force as well. Some people find excitement through other people, in relationships and sex. Others need more of a thrill, and go hang-gliding or bungee-jumping, although the most common everyday outlet for sensation-seeking is reckless driving. My work has shown that people have a basic need for excitement—and one way or another, they will fulfill it.

How does your character find excitement? What risks does he take—and, perhaps more importantly, what risks would he *like* to take?

Did You Know?

Who displays the riskiest behaviors? Zuckerman explained:

> The greatest risk-takers are young males in their adolescent years—a fact reflected in their high rates of auto accidents, binge drinking, drug use and

pathological gambling. The military has always preferred younger men for soldiers, not only because of their physical strength but for their willingness to risk their lives in combat.

If your character is a young male and he *isn't* taking some risks, then that, too, speaks volumes about his character.

Food For Thought

• What sort of character would never go on a road adventure?

• What sort of character is always itching for a road adventure?

• Under what circumstances would your character drop everything and go off on an adventure?

SCENARIO NO. 16

AT THE SEX SHOP

Your character has passed a certain sex shop many times without dropping in. Today, for some reason (try to get the reason in mind), she decides to step inside. Picture the shop's part of town, the time of day, your character's emotions as she considers entering and then does enter, and the details of the shop's interior and merchandise (if you can't picture those, you may have to make a visit!).

At the same time, think through your character's sexual history, sexual interests, and current sex life. Is your character comfortable or uncomfortable making love? Does she have a high sex drive, medium sex drive, or low sex drive? Is your character heterosexual, homosexual, or bisexual? Has your character had certain formative sexual experiences that have colored or molded how she views sex? Use this scenario to investigate your character's relationship to her sexual nature.

· ·

1. Does your character visit sex shops:

  A) Frequently?
  B) Regularly?
  C) Sometimes?

D) Rarely?

E) Never?

. . . .

A) Visiting sex shops frequently is consistent with a character with sexual addiction tendencies who obsesses about sex, binds anxiety through sexual activity, and needs near-constant sexual stimulation.

B) Visiting sex shops regularly is consistent with a character who needs a lot of novelty in her partnered and autoerotic sex life and is likely an adventurous risk-taker in all walks of life.

C) Sometimes visiting sex shops is consistent with a character who is free enough to ignore society's taboos about frequenting such shops but whose modest needs and desires do not provoke regular visits.

D) Rarely visiting sex shops is consistent with a mature, well-adjusted character who maintains a satisfying sex life without the need for very many toys or additional stimulation but who occasionally feels the urge to get her or her partner a treat.

E) Never visiting sex shops is consistent with a repressed, conventional character who may be afraid of sexual activity or afraid of what she might unleash if she tapped into her sexual energy and nature.

How often does your character visit sex shops?

. . . .  . . . .

2. Why does your character drop into the sex shop?

A) Idle curiosity?

B) Out of something like revulsion?

C) To buy a gift for her sex partner?

D) To buy a gift for herself?

E) Because she has a fetish?

. . . .

A) Dropping into the sex shop out of idle curiosity is consistent with a character who likes to explore what life has to offer and who is inclined to live dangerously—or at least to think about living dangerously.

B) Dropping into the sex shop out of something like revulsion is consistent with a character brought up on harsh religious dogma about the sinfulness of sex, who may have been sexually abused in childhood, and who finds sexual activity a source of torment and high anxiety.

c) Dropping in to buy a gift for her sex partner is consistent with a playful character who likes a lot of novelty in her life or, alternatively, with a controlling character who likes to take charge of her sex life and make demands on her partner.

D) Dropping in to buy a gift for herself is consistent with a self-assured character who is comfortable with autoeroticism and feels free to take care of her basic sexual needs.

E) Dropping in because she has a fetish is consistent with a character prone to obsessions and addictions who may, because of early trauma, find ordinary sexual arousal difficult or even impossible.

Why does your character drop into the sex shop?

3. What is your character's primary emotion as she enters the sex shop?

  A) Embarrassment?
  B) Guilt?
  c) Fear?
  D) Curiosity?
  E) Excitement?

A) Experiencing embarrassment is consistent with a shy, self-conscious character who is uncomfortable talking about sex and who may be uncomfortable with any but the most usual sexual practices.

B) Experiencing guilt is consistent with an anxious, rule-bound character with a negative self-image and low self-esteem whose self-talk is on the punitive and self-disparaging side.

c) Experiencing fear is consistent with a repressed, probably traumatized character who likely grew up in a harsh, punitive environment where she was lectured about the immorality of sex while being sexually exploited.

D) Experiencing curiosity is consistent with a mature, well-adjusted character who likes to explore life and explore sex with or without a sexual partner.

E) Experiencing enthusiasm is consistent with a rebellious, passionate character who prides herself on living on the fringes of society and frequenting places like this sex shop.

What is your character's primary emotion upon entering the sex shop?

4. The brash-talking clerk's first words to your character are, "So, what gets you off?" How does your character respond?

   A) By blushing and turning away?
   B) By angrily replying, "None of your business!"?
   C) By innocently replying, "I'm not really sure."?
   D) By slyly replying, "What do you recommend?"?
   E) By acting indifferent and waving the question away?

A) Blushing and turning away is consistent with a shy, self-conscious character who is likely disturbed by her own self-consciousness and who shuns social situations because of her awkwardness and anxious feelings.

B) Replying angrily is consistent with a repressed, conventional, and probably traumatized character who displaces her anger on the clerk when in fact she is furious with her abusive parents and the abusive lovers she has allowed into her life.

C) Replying innocently is consistent with a naïve character who may find herself exploited in a variety of situations, from the social to the sexual to the financial.

D) Replying slyly is consistent with an intelligent, adventurous character who likes to play games in life, including sexual games, and who experiences a rich and varied inner life.

E) Acting indifferent is consistent with a proud, ironic character who makes a point of not showing her true feelings and who appears cool and aloof, even though she may be burning inside.

How does your character respond to the clerk's sexually explicit remark?

...............................⁜...............................

5. An attractive stranger strikes up a conversation with your character as they examine the same sex toys. Does your character:

    A) Move away out of embarrassment?
    B) Respond suspiciously?
    c) Act worldly and cool?
    D) Respond seductively?
    E) Respond matter-of-factly?

....

A) Moving away out of embarrassment is consistent with a self-effacing character whose first impulse is to recede into the shadows and who likely suffers from performance anxiety and other anxiety ailments.

B) Responding suspiciously is consistent with mildly paranoid character who may have been burned enough times to now choose discretion over excitement.

c) Acting worldly and cool is consistent with a self-conscious character who likes to adopt poses and who likely is slow to reveal her true nature and her true intentions.

D) Responding seductively is consistent with a flirtatious character who enjoys sex and sexual encounters or, alternatively, with a character who was abused in childhood and now responds seductively as a result of that childhood abuse.

E) Responding matter-of-factly is consistent with a self-assured character who has had enough relational experience, both good and bad, to take a new opportunity for romance in stride.

What does your character do when an attractive stranger strikes up a conversation in the sex shop?

...............................⁜...............................

6. Your character is thinking about making a purchase but finds herself hesitating because:

A) She feels too embarrassed to take the item to the check-out counter?

B) She is a little repulsed by the idea of actually using the item?

C) It feels like too much of an extravagance?

D) She doubts that the item would ever get any use?

E) She is afraid what her partner would think or say?

• •

A) Hesitating out of embarrassment is consistent with a self-conscious character who, because of her anxiety issues, likely avoids many opportunities for adventure, enjoyment, and growth.

B) Hesitating out of repulsion is consistent with a squeamish character who is likely burdened by inner prohibitions against self-gratification and physical enjoyment.

C) Hesitating because of the price is consistent with a frugal character who is likely careful and contained in all of her dealings and interactions.

D) Hesitating because she doubts that the item would get used is consistent with a pessimistic character who purchased enough gym memberships and diet aids to know how often she fails to follow through on her intentions.

E) Hesitating out of a fear of her partner's reaction is consistent with an anxious, dependent character who regularly gives away her power to the people in her life.

If she does, why does your character hesitate before buying the sex toy that interests her?

Situations to Consider

What would your character do if:

- Someone she knew entered the store?
- The sex toy that intrigued her came with a prominent danger warning?
- She had a question about a sex toy?
- The clerk presented her with a mailing list to sign?
- She noticed, on the shop's bulletin board, an open invitation to a sex party that evening?
- She had a question about a sexual practice?

- She began to suspect that one of the customers was an undercover cop?

Other Sex-Related Situations

Put your character in the most appropriate of the following situations and think through how she would act and react. If you like, flesh out the scene by adding one conflict and one surprise.

- a visit to a strip club
- an invitation to an orgy
- a sexual encounter while traveling
- an evening among sadomasochists
- a bondage-and-discipline event
- a surprise encounter with a former lover
- a surprise encounter with a transvestite

Androgyny and Sex Role Stereotyping

Typically, a character in a novel is either clearly masculine or clearly feminine. In real life, human beings manifest a lot of masculine and feminine qualities. In 1974, Stanford University psychologist Sandra Bem elaborated the age-old concept of androgyny: The androgynous person is high in both masculine and feminine traits and can be aggressive or yielding, forceful or gentle, sensitive or assertive as the situation requires. In feminist and queer theoretical writings, the term often denotes a subversive alternative to a rigidly defined system of sex/gender differences.

Androgyny is sometimes celebrated as a liberating vision of wholeness through the blurring or breaking down of false gender categories. But despite our fascination with androgyny and the many real-life examples of androgyny, most people (including most readers) tend to think in terms of sex role stereotypes: They expect men to display certain qualities and traits and women to display a different set of qualities and traits.

Psychology professor David A. Gershaw explained in an article titled "Androgyny: Masculine & Feminine":

> Our gender roles affect almost every aspect of our lives, but few of us spend much time thinking about them. If a man cries at times, is he less masculine? If a woman tries to assert herself, is she less feminine? In most cultures, there are distinct roles for men and women. However, the roles vary from culture to culture.

In the United States, there is a consensus on the stereotyped roles for the average man or woman. The traits in these stereotypes fall into two separate groups. The first expresses competence and independence, while the second focuses on warmth and expressiveness. Men are seen as having the competence traits, while women are seen as more expressive.

Men are viewed as appropriately aggressive, independent, dominant, competitive, and ambitious, and women are viewed as appropriately tactful, quiet, desirous of security, easily able to express their feelings, and aware of the feelings of other people. So if your character is male and not competitive, we are inclined not to see him as a real man, and if she is blunt and unconcerned about the feelings of other people, we are not inclined to see her as a real woman.

Is your character more aligned with her sex role stereotype or more in opposition to it? Is she an androgynous mix of qualities—or even someone who celebrates androgyny?

Did You Know?

There is almost nothing that somebody doesn't find sexually arousing. Here are a dozen less-than-common sexual fetishes (from the hundreds that a comprehensive list would include):

CRATING: S&M practice in which a master packs her slave in a crate and sends him to friends by post

DISNEY/TOONS: Disney or other commercial cartoon characters depicted engaging in sexual activities

EMETOPHILIA: arousal from vomit or vomiting

FURRIES: arousal through dressing up in an animal costume

GIANTESS: fetish involving imaginary giant women

HARPAXOPHILIA: arousal from being robbed

K/S: Erotic material featuring the original Star Trek main characters Kirk and Spock having sex with each other

LOOSE SOCKS: aroused by Japanese schoolgirls with loose socks

MEDICAL: fetish about nurses/doctors and medical exams or equipment

PONY PLAY: sexual practice involving people being treated as horses

TAPHEPHILIA: arousal from being buried alive

TRAMPLE: being stepped on by large or heavy people, often many people or very heavy objects (for example, cars)

If your character had an unusual sexual fetish, what would it be?

Food for Thought

• Does your character consider herself sexually attractive or sexually unattractive?

• Under what circumstances (if any) would your character engage in unsafe sex?

• To whom is your character most sexually attracted?

SCENARIO NO. 17
DEATHBED SECRET

Imagine that your character learns an important, potentially life-changing secret at the deathbed of a close relative. The secret might be that your character has a sibling about whom he has never heard a word, that his putative father is not really his biological father, that he is a racial mix, that he is adopted, or something of equivalent weight and moment. Let's take one of these to consider: that the man he has always presumed was his father is not, in fact, his biological father.

Picture your character at the deathbed of this relative (let's make him an uncle). Get the details in mind: the lightness or darkness of the room, the flowers or absence of flowers, the hush or noise, the quality of the interaction, the manner in which the secret is revealed. Then consider the following questions.

1. What is your character's first reaction upon hearing this news?

    A) Shock and disbelief?
    B) Indifference?
    C) Anger?
    D) Sadness?
    E) Relief?

A) Experiencing shock and disbelief are natural, unremarkable reactions. Experiencing extreme shock and disbelief (say, by fainting) is consistent with a naïve character who looks at the world through rose-colored glasses and is dismayed by the seamy side of human affairs.

B) Experiencing indifference is consistent with a worldly, self-assured character who prides himself on not being affected by anything or anyone.

C) Experiencing anger is a natural, unremarkable reaction. Experiencing extreme anger is consistent with a volatile character whose anger may in fact be rooted in a long-standing, half-aware knowledge of this very secret.

D) Experiencing sadness is a natural, unremarkable reaction. Experiencing extreme sadness is consistent with an emotionally fragile, possibly depressed character whose pessimistic outlook and low self-esteem will be badly exacerbated by this new blow.

E) Experiencing relief is consistent with a self-aware, intuitive character who senses when things aren't right and who has long been suspicious that the family was keeping a secret from him.

What is your character's first reaction upon hearing this news?

2. How does your character overtly react in the moment?

    A) Sit in stunned silence?
    B) Dispute the veracity of the news?
    C) React emotionally with anger?
    D) React emotionally with tears?
    E) Press for more information?

A) Sitting in stunned silence is consistent with a character who is easily overwhelmed, finds life already daunting, and is unlikely to possess the inner resources to deal effectively with this news.

B) Disputing the veracity of the news is consistent with a character whose primary defense mechanism is denial and who likely spends a considerable portion of his life living in fantasy and refusing to believe the evidence of his own senses.

c) Reacting emotionally with anger is consistent with a strong, self-contained character who refuses to be treated unjustly or, alternatively, with an angry, perhaps violent character who is likely controlling and quick to walk out of relationships.

D) Reacting emotionally with tears is consistent with a character whose pent-up emotions are regularly near the surface and who, even if he can usually keep those emotions in check, may be more agitated and troubled than he realizes.

E) Pressing for more information is consistent with a solid, courageous character who prefers knowing to not knowing, even when the news is bad, and who likely thinks matters through before deciding on how he wants to proceed.

How does your character overtly react in the moment?

3. What does your character do after leaving his uncle?

  A) Confront his mother?
  B) Confront his father?
  c) Interrogate other family members?
  D) Retire to his room to think?
  E) Go out and drink?

A) Confronting his mother is consistent with a character who has had long-simmering conflicts with his mother and who may have grown up in a household where verbal tirades, emotional confrontations, and intense interactions were everyday affairs.

B) Confronting his father is consistent with a forceful character who is not afraid to stand up to patriarchal energy and who sees himself as less the dutiful child and more the equal adult.

c) Interrogating other family members is consistent with a confident character who is unembarrassed to speak the truth in order to gain more information or, alternatively, with an angry character who needs to know which other family members have been withholding, so as to give them a piece of his mind.

D) Retiring to his room to think is consistent with an intelligent character with a brooding nature who likely stews about matters, runs conversations in his mind, and keeps a running journal or diary of his thoughts.

E) Going out and drinking is consistent with an impulsive character who meets life's challenges by self-medicating and who is likely to display addictive tendencies in a variety of ways, including in his relationships.

What does your character do after leaving his uncle?

4. Do his interactions with his father change? Does he:

    A) Become more distant?
    B) Become more hostile?
    C) Become more evasive?
    D) Become more loving?
    E) Become more uninterested?

A) Becoming more distant is consistent with a troubled character who has withdrawn into his shell, is likely depressed, and who may live in a fantasy world of soap operas, sports shows, or Internet surfing so as to mask and minimize the pain he is feeling.

B) Becoming more hostile is consistent with a character who expresses sadness and hurt feelings through anger and is likely always at war with someone, whether acquaintance, friend, or family member.

C) Becoming more evasive is consistent with a character who has decided that people can't be trusted and that self-protection demands doing unto others before they do unto him.

D) Becoming more loving is consistent with a character who is able to empathize, forgive, feel compassion, and acknowledge that human beings come with shortcomings as well as strengths.

E) Becoming more uninterested is consistent with a character who has made peace with this particular injustice or, alternatively, with a character who has decided to write off certain people in his life.

How do your character's interactions with his putative father change?

5. Over time, what is his reaction to the news?

    A) Progressively more divorced from his family?
    B) Progressively more obsessed about his biological father?
    C) Progressively more depressed?
    D) Progressively angrier about the news?
    E) Progressively more adjusted to the news?

A) Becoming progressively more divorced from his family is consistent with a character who is wrestling with issues of autonomy and independence, and who believes that in order to gain that autonomy he should keep a strict distance between himself and his parents.

B) Becoming progressively more obsessed about his biological father is consistent with a character who is unsure of himself and who presumes that he will learn something important about who he really is by getting to know his real father.

C) Becoming progressively more depressed is consistent with a troubled character who was already significantly depressed and for whom this news was a further—even a final—humiliating blow.

D) Becoming progressively angrier about the news is consistent with a volatile and perhaps impulsive character who is full of rage or, alternatively, with a character with a fine-tuned sense of justice who, the more he thinks about it, grows angrier at the perceived injustice.

E) Becoming progressively more adjusted to the news is consistent with a strong, self-confident, and secure character who was naturally thrown for a loop when he first heard the news but who ultimately assimilates the news and recovers from the blow with the passage of time.

Over time, what is your character's reaction to the news?

6. How is this news likely to affect your character's self-image?

    A) Significantly tarnish his self-image?
    B) Moderately tarnish his self-image?

c) Slightly tarnish his self-image?

d) Leave his self-image unaffected?

e) Improve his self-image?

● ●

A) The news significantly tarnishing his self-image is consistent with a character who already had self-esteem and self-confidence issues, and for whom this may be a final blow that prevents him from achieving his goals and realizing his dreams.

B) The news moderately tarnishing his self-image is consistent with a character who has previously kept his conflicting feelings of worth and worthlessness in dynamic balance and who now has been thrown out of balance as a result of this revelation.

c) The news slightly tarnishing his self-image is consistent with a character who possesses significant strengths in the areas of self-confidence and self-esteem but who is just wounded enough that news of this magnitude causes a real—but perhaps only temporary—decline.

D) The news leaving his self-image unaffected is consistent with a strong, self-confident character who feels completely separate from (and perhaps superior to) his parents and who, because of his strength and autonomy, is unaffected by this ostensibly disturbing development.

E) The news improving his self-image is consistent with a character who had an inkling that things were not right in his life, who is now gratified to learn that his intuition was correct, and who has been made stronger by having his intuition validated.

How is the news likely to affect your character's self-image?

Situations to Consider

What would your character do if:

- He always had doubts about his paternity?
- He knew this uncle to be a liar?
- He knew this uncle hated his father?
- His father was dying?
- His mother and father were talking about divorcing?
- He loved his father enormously?
- He suspected the identity of his biological father?

Other Life-Changing Situations

Put your character in the most appropriate of the following situations and think through how he would act and react. If you like, flesh out the scene by adding one conflict and one surprise.

- news about a hitherto unknown sibling
- news that he is adopted
- news that he is biracial
- news of a family scandal
- news of a family fortune
- news that his parents never married
- news of a genetic family illness

Resilience

Some people seem to be able to bounce back more easily and more completely than other people. How resilient does your character seem to you? Confronted by a secret as important as the ones described in this scenario, will your character remain relatively unaffected, have a breakdown, or display an amount of resilience midway along the continuum?

One important factor is a person's network of relationships. According to a brochure titled "The Road to Resilience" released by the American Psychological Association (www.apahelpcenter.org):

> Many studies show that the primary factor in resilience is having caring and supportive relationships within and outside the family. Relationships that create love and trust, provide role models, and offer encouragement and reassurance help bolster a person's resilience.

Did You Know?

You can show that the tide is turning for your character by the way he begins to see crisis as opportunity. According to the APA:

> You can't change the fact that highly stressful events happen, but you can change how you interpret and respond to these events. Try looking beyond the present to how future circumstances may be a little better. Note any subtle ways in which you might already feel somewhat better as you deal with difficult situations.

What sort of opportunity might learning a secret of the sort provide for your character?

Food for Thought

• What sort of revelation would really shake your character up?

• What sort of revelation that might shake someone else up wouldn't affect your character at all?

• Does your character possess a secret that, if revealed, would profoundly affect others?

SCENARIO NO. 18
STALKED

Your character is being stalked. First, create the events leading up to the stalking. Perhaps your character works in an office and is now being stalked by a recently fired coworker. Maybe your character is a celebrity and is being stalked by a fan. Maybe your character is being stalked by a former lover or an estranged spouse. Think through what stalking situation is most likely in your character's case or, alternatively, would give you the most to chew on.

Once you've decided on the circumstances, get the details clearly in mind. What does the stalker look like? How does she behave? Does the stalker keep his distance or confront your character? How dangerous does the stalker seem? Picture in vivid detail your character being stalked and then proceed to the following questions.

1. What is your character's main reaction to being stalked?

   A) Fear?
   B) Anger?
   C) Annoyance?
   D) Curiosity?
   E) Indifference?

A) Reacting fearfully is consistent with an anxious, fearful character who has suffered previous traumas and who is very alert to, and even paranoid about, the presence of threats in her life.

B) Reacting with anger is consistent with a strong, self-confident character who is not used to countenancing threats and who is likely to confront threats head-on when they occur.

C) Reacting with annoyance is consistent with a busy, rushed, perhaps unaware character who doesn't fully recognize threats, whether they are threats to her health (from obesity or smoking), threats to her relationships, or threats to her physical safety.

D) Reacting with curiosity is consistent with a naïve character who is quick to see the good in people and quick to downplay the possibility of threat or, alternatively, with an intelligent, educated, ironic character who, out of boredom, finds anything unusual, even being stalked, amusing and interesting.

E) Reacting with indifference is consistent with a defeated, downtrodden, depressed character who doesn't care about her physical safety and who may even welcome danger as a respite from depression.

What is your character's main reaction to being stalked?

2. Does your character:

   A) Angrily confront the stalker?
   B) Try to reason with the stalker?
   C) Try to ignore the stalker?
   D) Try to hide from the stalker?
   E) Call the police?

A) Angrily confronting the stalker is consistent with a volatile personality whose first reaction to conflict is anger or, alternatively, with a powerful, self-confident character who is unused to being threatened and refuses to countenance it.

B) Trying to reason with the stalker is consistent with a self-contained character who is used to employing interpersonal skills in dealing with conflicts or, alternatively, with a naïve character who doesn't realize what little positive effect rationality will have on an irrational stalker.

c) Trying to ignore the stalker is consistent with a character who lacks self-awareness and tries to ignore life's problems or, alternatively, with an optimistic character who is generally hopeful and hopes that this problem will resolve itself of its own accord.

D) Trying to hide from the stalker is consistent with a timid, fearful character who feels unequal to meeting threats, has been significantly harmed before, and doesn't feel in possession of the emotional or practical resources necessary to deal with a stalker.

E) Calling the police is consistent with a straightforward, matter-of-fact character who is used to directly dealing with problems and who expects people in authority, like the police, to do their job and rectify problems of this sort.

How does your character try to deal with the stalker?

3. The stalker sends your character a love letter. Does your character:

    A) Tear it up?
    B) Save it as evidence?
    c) Write back angrily?
    D) Write back and try to reason?
    E) Show it to others?

A) Tearing the love letter up is consistent with a character who may be annoyed by the stalker's attention and irritated at having to deal with a problem of this sort but who hasn't registered this as a real threat and who supposes that not responding will end this unwanted interaction.

B) Saving the love letter as evidence is consistent with a frightened character who is used to carefully paying her bills on time, watching her diet, and managing her anxiety through obsessive and compulsive attention to details.

c) Writing back angrily (should a return address be given) is consistent with a thin-skinned, impulsive character who tends to pour fuel on fires and shares in the responsibility for creating the dramas in her life.

D) Writing back and trying to reason with the stalker is consistent with a naïve character who is unaware that communication is likely to escalate the threat or, alternatively, with a character who unconsciously likes the attention and wants the drama to continue.

E) Showing the love letter to others is consistent with a practical, self-confident character who likes to elicit advice before taking action or, alternatively, with a character who lacks self-confidence and needs input from others in order to make decisions.

What does your character do upon receiving a love letter from the stalker?

4. The stalker communicates to your character that he will stop the pursuit if your character joins him for just one drink. How does your character respond?

    A) Flatly refuses?
    B) Says she will think about it?
    C) Agrees but doesn't go?
    D) Agrees and goes?
    E) Agrees and goes, but brings a friend?

A) Flatly refusing is consistent with a savvy, self-confident character who is able to say no in life and who realizes that any interaction with a stalker, whether the interaction is hostile or friendly, is likely to cause the stalking to persist.

B) Thinking about it is consistent with a careful, perhaps timid character who is likely indecisive and may ultimately act impulsively, perhaps agreeing to the meeting at the last minute even though she has been planning all along to refuse.

C) Agreeing but not going is consistent with a character who has trouble telling the truth and whose modus operandi is to act agreeable, make arrangements and commitments, and then not follow through, often without offering up an explanation or excuse.

D) Agreeing and going is consistent with a courageous character who believes that she can end this pursuit through a face-to-face meeting or, alternatively, with a naïve character who misunderstands the level of disturbance implied by stalking and won't be prepared for the crises to follow.

E) Agreeing and going, but bringing a friend, is consistent with a character who is used to soliciting support from friends and who may make unwise decisions because she feels protected when in the company of her friends.

How does your character respond to the stalker's invitation to join him for a drink?

5. Your character discovers that the stalker has entered her house while she was out. Does your character:

  A) Immediately call the police?
  B) Feel numb and paralyzed?
  C) Pour herself a few stiff drinks?
  D) Decide to confront the stalker?
  E) Spend the night with a friend or relative?

A) Immediately calling the police is consistent with a sensible, straightforward character who knows a break-in when she sees one and who is not hesitant to act decisively when the situation calls for decisive action.

B) Feeling numb and paralyzed is consistent with a timid, anxious, and perhaps distraught character who has trouble making decisions and who feels alone and unprotected with nowhere to turn.

C) Pouring herself a few stiff drinks is consistent with a character who manages anxiety with drugs and who might be expected to enter a period of heavy situational drinking as a result of the stalking and the break-in.

D) Deciding to confront the stalker is consistent with an impulsive, perhaps naïve character who doesn't appreciate the nature of this threat or, alternatively, with a forceful character who is used to taking matters into her own hands and feels physically equal to dealing with this problem.

E) Spending the night with a friend or relative is consistent with a fragile, cautious character who feels unequal to dealing with this threat alone and who looks for comfort and support from among her friends and relatives.

What does your character do upon learning that the stalker has entered her house?

6. The stalker suddenly vanishes. What is your character's first reaction?

   A) Suspicion?
   B) Fear?
   C) Relief?
   D) Curiosity?
   E) Indifference?

A) Reacting with suspicion is consistent with a world-wise, perhaps mildly paranoid character who suspects that this is the latest salvo in a war of nerves and perhaps even signals an escalation of the conflict rather than a cessation of hostilities.

B) Reacting with fear is consistent with an anxious character who fantasizes difficulties and who is as troubled by shadows and what isn't there as by literal threats and palpable dangers.

C) Reacting with relief is consistent with a character who dislikes dramas and difficulties, is eager to return to her normal routine, and is capable of experiencing gratitude when something good happens.

D) Reacting with curiosity is consistent with a thoughtful, intelligent character who is interested in human nature and human dynamics and as curious about why this stalking has suddenly ended as why it began in the first place.

E) Reacting with indifference is consistent with a bored character who hardly notices what's going on, is mildly depressed, and who takes little pleasure in her normal pursuits.

What is your character's first reaction upon noticing that the stalker has disappeared?

Situations to Consider

What would your character do if:

   • The stalker began stalking a loved one?
   • The stalker threatened violence?
   • The stalker looked intoxicated?

- The stalker reappeared after an absence?
- She was informed by the police that the best thing to do was to move?
- The stalker was joined by another stalker?
- Your character possessed a firearm?

Other Dangerous Situations

Put your character in the most appropriate of the following situations and think through how she would act and react. If you like, flesh out the scene by adding one conflict and one surprise.

- a material witness against mobsters
- a soldier during battle
- a traveler alone in a hostile environment
- a stranger in a rough bar
- a victim of identity theft
- a hostage in a holdup
- a passer-by in a mob scene

Stalker Traits

According to the organization End Stalking in America (www.esia.net):

- Stalkers will go to great lengths to obtain information about their victims and have been known to hack into computers, tap telephone lines, and take jobs at public utilities that allow them access to information about the victim.

- Stalkers many times have a mean streak and will become violent when frustrated. How violent? Often deadly.

Did You Know?

Here are some common mistakes that victims of stalkers make, again according to End Stalking in America:

- Not listening to their intuition that something might be wrong.

- Letting someone down easy rather than saying a definitive no if they're not interested in the relationship.

- Taking inadequate privacy and safety precautions.

- Neglecting to enlist the support of family, friends, neighbors, coworkers, therapists, and other victims.

Food for Thought

• When confronted by danger, is your character likely to act alone or to seek help?

• Under what circumstances would your character arm herself?

• Under what circumstances, if any, would your character become a stalker?

SCENARIO NO. 19
A VERY BUSY DAY

Your character is experiencing an unusually hectic day full of appointments, tasks, meetings, or whatever other kinds of duties and activities make sense in your character's case. If your character is a surgeon, imagine a day of nonstop, difficult surgeries punctuated by nonstop phone calls and e-mail. If your character is a police detective, imagine a day of nonstop crimes punctuated by personal dramas and special pressures. If your character is an architect, picture a day leading up to an important competition, with his whole firm's future on the line.

Get your character's hectic, pressurized day clearly in mind. Start him out in the morning on the run and do not let him stop running. Feel the stress, the demands, the impossibility of getting everything done. Flesh out the details, from checking e-mail to returning phone calls. Once you have your character's busy day clearly in mind, proceed to the following questions.

1. If this day is unusually busy because of something your character has done, what is that something?

A) Has he been slacking off and leaving things undone?

B) Has he been emotionally under the weather and not working at top speed?

C) Has he been focusing narrowly on one aspect of life or work and falling behind in other areas?

D) Has he inappropriately taken on too many tasks and responsibilities?

E) Is he unable to focus on the main tasks and consequently scurrying around tackling smaller tasks?

A) Slacking off and leaving things undone is consistent with a character who has mentally left his job out of boredom, indifference, or anger and is not only unconcerned about performing well but may even welcome being found out and put on notice.

B) Being emotionally under the weather and not working at top speed is consistent with a character who is experiencing a crisis, perhaps in his primary relationship, coupled with too many stresses, leading to emotional malaise and a partial inability to function.

C) Focusing narrowly on one aspect of life and falling behind in other areas is consistent with an anxious character who attempts to manage his anxiety by paying obsessive attention to that one area and who, as a result, makes big mistakes and messes in other areas of life.

D) Inappropriately taking on too many tasks and responsibilities is consistent with a character who has trouble saying no and whose self-image and self-worth are connected to needing to feel useful and even indispensable.

E) Not being able to focus and scurrying around with minor tasks are consistent with a character whose primary way of dealing with stress is to run faster and faster and who, by never stopping, can't muster the mind space to focus effectively on his larger tasks.

How has your character contributed to the busyness of this day?

2. What is your character's primary emotion as he rushes through this day?

A) Anxiety?

B) Irritation?
C) Anger?
D) Calmness?
E) Hopelessness?

••

A) Rushing through the day feeling anxious is consistent with a character who suffers from free-floating anxiety that settles on whatever is next on his plate or currently in his line of vision, coloring his days with vague but persistent uneasiness.

B) Rushing through the day feeling irritable is consistent with a character who is troubled by a particular unresolved conflict, for instance, an issue with his mate, and is consequently likely to criticize the people with whom he comes into contact.

C) Rushing through the day feeling angry is consistent with a character whose simmering grievances negatively color his life and may lead to temper tantrums and even acts of workplace violence.

D) Rushing through the day feeling calm is consistent with a character who has made a conscious choice to detach from worry, engages in a mindfulness practice like yoga or meditation, and knows that life's to-do list is never completed.

E) Rushing through the day feeling hopeless is consistent with a severely depressed character who lives life by going through the motions and who is likely hard-working and dependable but who experiences little pleasure or satisfaction from his activities and pursuits.

What is your character's primary emotion as he rushes through this day?

••••••••••••••••••••••••  •••••••••••••••••••••••••

3. Something out of your character's control slows down his day and threatens to derail it. Does he react:

A) Furiously?
B) Irritably?
C) Anxiously?
D) Histrionically?
E) Philosophically?

••

A) Acting furiously is consistent with an impulsive, volatile character whom other people, even his boss, tend to avoid and who is notorious around the office for flying off the handle.

B) Acting irritably is consistent with a self-involved, grandiose character who feels put upon and aggrieved and who may view the work he is doing as far beneath his dignity.

C) Acting anxiously is consistent with a fearful character who sees the end of the world in every minor setback, is the first to fear for his job, and is likely at least mildly phobic and superstitious.

D) Acting histrionically is consistent with a dramatic character who is easily thwarted, quick to blame others, and likely to have earned a deserved reputation as a drama king.

E) Acting philosophically is consistent with a mature, self-aware character who is comfortable in the knowledge that only so much in life can be controlled and that nothing is served by turning minor irritations into catastrophes.

How does your character react when something threatens to derail his day?

4. Your character has five minutes to spare between activities. Does he:

A) Check e-mail?
B) Glance at a newspaper?
C) Grab a PowerBar?
D) Stroll outside in the sun?
E) Stare blankly?

A) Checking e-mail is consistent with a nervous character who feels the need to keep himself busy at all times or, alternatively, with a hard-working, ambitious character who understands that to get everything done that he intends to get done requires making use of every spare minute.

B) Glancing at a newspaper is consistent with a character who feels compelled to keep up with the news, always feels more than a little behind, and is likely upset when someone seems to know more about world news and current events than he does.

c) Grabbing a PowerBar is consistent with a health-conscious, disciplined character who is likely to work out at the gym at dawn, take his job very seriously, and feel guilty if he doesn't make use of every available minute.

D) Strolling outside in the sun is consistent with a thoughtful, secure, and self-confident character who is able to take real breaks from work, smell the roses, and enter into a dreamy meditative state even in the middle of a hectic day.

E) Staring blankly is consistent with an overwhelmed, overworked character who is running from task to task on automatic pilot—and nearly on empty—and who has no reserve energy to muster for those rare moments when a task isn't pending.

What does your character do with five minutes to spare between activities?

5. Your character just can't do another thing. Does he:

    A) Ask for help?
    B) Take a quick break and return to work?
    c) Take a drink or pop a pill and return to work?
    D) Leave early?
    E) Just do it anyway?

A) Asking for help is consistent with a character who understands when he has taken on too much and who is able to swallow his pride and put the project first.

B) Taking a quick break and returning to work is consistent with a self-confident character who knows how to replenish his strength, make adjustments on the fly, and effectively meet life's demands, traits of the highly valued worker.

c) Taking a drink or popping a pill is consistent with a character who self-medicates in order to deal with stress and whose drug of choice likely reflects an aspect of character; a passive personality preferring marijuana;

an energetic personality preferring cocaine; a counter-culture, risk-taking personality preferring hallucinogenic drugs.

D) Leaving early is consistent with an emotionally fragile character whose modus operandi is to flee from stressful situations or, alternatively, with a sly, unreliable character who prefers to hide out and disappear when the stress level gets too high or when work begins to pile up.

E) Just doing it anyway is consistent with a strong-willed, disciplined character who is likely highly motivated and ambitious, and who likely periodically burns out as a result of uninterrupted stress and endless hard work.

What does your character do when he feels like it's not possible to do another thing?

6. At the end of this day, does your character:

    A) Have a quiet dinner with his mate?
    B) Rush off to a new round of activities?
    C) Stare moodily out the window?
    D) Drink heavily?
    E) Fall into bed early without even brushing his teeth?

A) Having a quiet dinner with his mate is consistent with a character who values intimate relationships, who is able to effectively decompress through sharing and relating, and who prefers simple, undramatic living to crises and theatrics.

B) Rushing off to a new round of activities is consistent with a character who races through life so as to avoid confronting his thoughts and feelings or, alternatively, with a character who is so full of energy that he is equal to burning the candle at both ends.

C) Staring moodily out the window is consistent with a troubled character who is unhappy with his life, both at work and at home, and who is on the brink of some dramatic action, whether that's quitting his job or something even more drastic.

D) Drinking heavily is consistent with a character with addictive tendencies who drinks to deal with stress, who may be in one or another stage of alcoholic drinking, and who is unlikely to be able to maintain his current level of functioning.

E) Falling into bed early is consistent with a character who is barely managing to meet his obligations and who can only meet them by spending his time away from work recovering from the current day and physically and emotionally preparing for the next day.

What does your character do at the end of a day of this sort?

Situations to Consider

What would your character do if:

- He was told by his boss to be more productive?
- He began having small accidents at work?
- He began having stomach pains at work?
- He started making big mistakes at work?
- He fell completely behind at work, despite working fourteen hours a day?
- He were confronted by a new, large task, on top of everything else?
- He started yelling at people at work?

Other Rushed Situations

Put your character in the most appropriate of the following situations and think through how he would act and react. If you like, flesh out the scene by adding one conflict and one surprise.

- preparing for a family vacation
- preparing to sell the house
- a week with many out-of-town visitors
- the first days of a new job
- a week with many evening commitments
- approaching deadline on the rollout of a product
- preparing a wedding

Time-Impatience and Free-Floating Hostility

Many people live life not only on the run but on the run in a characteristically pressurized and intense way that's given rise to the concept of the Type A personality. Two traits of the Type A personality are time-impatience and free-floating hostility. In "Characteristics of 'Type A' Personality," an article published by Mind Publications (www.mindpub.com), psychologist Vijai Sharma provided a set of informal questions to assess for these two traits.

Answering yes to the following suggests the presence of time-impatience:

- Do you eat fast and leave the dinner table immediately?
- Does your partner tell you to slow down or take it easy?
- Does it bother you a lot to have to wait in line?

Pervasive and ever-present hostility can be assessed by the following questions:

- Do you often find it difficult to fall asleep because you are upset about something a person has done?
- Do you become irritated when driving or swear at others?
- Do you grind your teeth or has your dentist ever told you that you have done so?

Is your character a Type A personality?

Did You Know?

The Type A personality tends toward out-sized materialism. Type A's want to know how much you earn, what things cost, and what's in fashion. They tend to spend money as fast as they make it, and give money and gifts, rather than time and attention, as a way of showing affection. Money is their medium and materialism their religion.

Food for Thought

- Does your character essentially enjoy or hate keeping very busy?
- How busy is too busy for this particular character?
- What, if anything, has your character learned to do to slow down in life?

SCENARIO NO. 20
A MOMENT OF HIGH DRAMA

Out of the blue, your character is confronted by a moment of high drama. Depending on the nature of your character and your novel, choose one of the following dramatic moments: (1) caught in a major earthquake; (2) unjustly arrested for murder; (3) tailing the kidnapper of a child; or (4) watching a loved one die unexpectedly.

Get the incident clearly in mind. What was your character doing before the moment of high drama commenced? What was she feeling? Picture the drama unfolding: the building beginning to shake, your character feeling the handcuffs going on, your character noticing a man snatching a child, your character hearing the loved one's death rattle. Once you have the incident clearly in mind, proceed to the following questions.

1. What strength of character does your character manifest in this moment?

A) Courage?
B) Presence of mind?
C) Resolve?

D) Calmness?

E) Self-control?

. . . .

A) Manifesting courage is consistent with a character who takes pride in standing up and in not failing herself or, alternatively, with a socialized character who falls into step with the norms of society, which includes acting a certain way in emergencies.

B) Manifesting presence of mind is consistent with a character who is a natural leader in emergencies, knows useful skills like first aid and CPR, and can be expected to think through—and then make—any hard choices that may confront her.

C) Manifesting resolve is consistent with a character who has persevered through a lifetime of hard knocks and who has the self-awareness to recognize that in any situation, even the roughest, how she will react is in her control.

D) Manifesting calmness is consistent with a phlegmatic character with a low heart rate, slow movements, and a calculating nature who likes to think before she acts and prefers quiet to bustle.

E) Manifesting self-control is consistent with a character who has learned to manage anxiety through strictness and who knows how to ration scarce resources, denies herself treats, and is likely a fan of corporal punishment and of children being seen but not heard.

What strength of character does your character manifest in this moment?

. . . .  . . . .

2. What weakness of character does your character manifest in this moment?

A) Self-pity?

B) Cowardice?

C) Lack of resolve?

D) Mental confusion?

E) High anxiety?

. . . .

A) Manifesting self-pity is consistent with a self-indulgent, pampered character who is likely to whine, blame others, love material things, and lack empathy.

B) Manifesting cowardice is consistent with a secretive, grandiose character who feels both frightened and superior, and whose approach to danger is to hide and to let other inferior, disposable human beings do the dirty work and take the risks.

C) Manifesting lack of resolve is consistent with a blustery character who appears self-confident and can talk a good game but who is more anxious and frightened than she appears and who consequently falters in crunch time.

D) Manifesting mental confusion is consistent with a character who lacks real autonomy and independence, who likely thinks of herself as dumb, silly, or addled, and who leaves the decision-making process to others—like a mate or parents—while internally criticizing those decisions.

E) Manifesting high anxiety is consistent with a generally anxious character whose anxiety escalates in emergencies, reaching phobic proportions, and culminating in panic and hysteria.

What weakness of character does your character manifest in this moment?

3. Your character has to make a big decision (to continue following the kidnapper or to stop and call the police, to talk to the police, to demand a lawyer, and so on). Does she make the decision:

A) With great trepidation?
B) Anxiously and uncertainly?
C) Recklessly and impulsively?
D) Thoughtfully?
E) Blankly, as if in a trance?

A) Acting with great trepidation is consistent with a character who lacks self-confidence, is likely swayed by the opinions of others and feels judged by others, and tends to meet emergencies with paralysis and inaction.

B) Acting anxiously and uncertainly is consistent with a meek character who has led a sheltered, reclusive life, has tried to put herself in the position of avoiding making difficult decisions, and is likely to second-guess her decision afterward.

c) Acting recklessly and impulsively is consistent with an immature character who acts first and thinks later, takes needless risks, is a danger to herself and to others, and likely has had a few scrapes with the law.

D) Acting thoughtfully is consistent with an intelligent, self-confident, self-contained character who possesses the emotional and intellectual resources to calmly appraise her options even in life-threatening circumstances.

E) Acting blankly, as if in a trance, is consistent with a character whose anxiety manifests itself as mental confusion and who likely spaces out in stressful situations, whether the stressful situation is taking a test, interviewing for a job, or reacting in an emergency.

How does your character make an important decision during a moment of high drama?

4. The situation worsens (not only has a loved one died but your character is in danger herself, and so on). Does the worsening situation:

    A) Increase your character's resolve?
    B) Put your character in a panic?
    c) Cause your character to shut down mentally and physically?
    D) Arouse your character's ire?
    E) Cause your character to give up?

A) Reacting with increased resolve is consistent with a strong, self-reliant character whose resources become more mobilized as a situation worsens and who likely lands in leadership positions.

B) Panicking is consistent with a character whose emotional and mental resources can be stretched thin by circumstances and who can be brought to the breaking point by too many simultaneous stresses.

c) Shutting down mentally and physically is consistent with a character who lacks self-awareness, doesn't recognize when anxiety and stress are taking their toll, and tends to react to emergencies with denial and paralysis.

D) Reacting with irritation and anger is consistent with a passionate, powerful character who gets stronger as problems worsen or, alternatively, with an immature, impulsive character who feels put upon, blames the world for her problems, and handles emergencies with temper tantrums.

E) Giving up is consistent with a character who has experienced multiple traumas in life, feels unequal to handling life's challenges, and likely has a history of abandoning people, pursuits, and professions.

How would your character react if the situation worsened?

5. In the middle of this moment of high drama something trivial happens (your character stubs a toe, breaks a nail, and so on). How does your character react?

    A) With disproportionate anger?
    B) With disproportionate anxiety?
    C) With disproportionate sadness?
    D) Without noticing it at all?
    E) By taking it in stride?

A) Reacting with disproportionate anger is consistent with a character who has poor impulse control, regularly lashes out at strangers and intimates alike, and likely has an addictive nature associated with overeating, promiscuity, and/or alcohol and drug abuse.

B) Reacting with disproportionate anxiety is consistent with a generally anxious character who likely manifests physical symptoms of anxiety like insomnia, irritable bowel syndrome, or stomachaches, and mental symptoms of anxiety like confusion and indecisiveness.

C) Reacting with disproportionate sadness is consistent with a depressed character with a melancholy nature who likely has suffered many disappointments and defeats, who feels isolated and alienated, and who has trouble coming up with reasons for living.

D) Not noticing it at all is consistent with an overburdened, perpetually rushing character who misses much of what is happening around her, lacks self-awareness, and is prone to frequent accidents and mishaps.

E) Taking it in stride is consistent with a self-confident, phlegmatic character with the cognitive self-control not to make mountains out of molehills and the ability to reason rather than react.

How would your character react if something trivial happened in the middle of this moment of high drama?

· 🎭 ·

6. In the middle of this moment of high drama, your character makes a serious mistake (lets the kidnapper get too far ahead, accidentally incriminates herself, and so on). How does your character react in the moment?

    A) With self-loathing?
    B) With high anxiety?
    c) With guilty feelings?
    D) With anger?
    E) With self-forgiveness?

· ·

A) Reacting with self-loathing is consistent with a character with low self-esteem and a poor self-image who is prone to powerful feelings of shame and is likely the victim of self-sabotaging behaviors, for instance, cutting and self-mutilation.

B) Reacting with high anxiety is consistent with a timid character who worries about how others will judge her for making the mistake or obsesses about the worst-case scenario resulting from the mistake.

c) Reacting with guilty feelings is consistent with a character who likely was criticized as a child, who internally takes the blame for matters not in her control, and who doubts that anything she does is ever really appreciated.

D) Reacting with anger is consistent with a volatile, passionate character who likely has hearty appetites, takes risks, and prefers to live life large.

E) Reacting with self-forgiveness is consistent with a secure, self-confident character who does not like making mistakes and probably makes fewer mistakes than the average person but who understands that mistakes are an inevitable part of living.

How would your character react to making a serious mistake during this moment of high drama?

Situations to Consider

What would your character do if:

- This moment of high drama was followed by another of equal intensity and difficulty?
- A side drama erupted?
- In the middle of this drama, someone turned to your character for help?
- The intensity, danger, or difficulty persisted for many days?
- A year later, the same drama repeated itself?
- Your character felt herself losing her grip?
- Your character began irrationally blaming herself for causing the drama?

Other High Drama Situations

Put your character in the most appropriate of the following situations and think through how she would act and react. If you like, flesh out the scene by adding one conflict and one surprise.

- ship sinking
- airplane nose-diving
- impending enemy attack
- cross-examined on the witness stand
- meeting a biological parent for the first time
- hotel fire
- confronting a child about his drug use

Effects of Bombing on Soldiers in Battle

You are a soldier in battle. You find yourself under bombardment. That is one sort of moment of high drama. What if the bombardment stops, then resumes? Are the psychological effects on you different then? The research on this question has produced two contradictory answers: that renewed bombardment increases your anxiety and that renewed bombardment begins to desensitize you to the danger.

In "Psychological Effects of Aerial Bombardment," published in *Airpower Journal*, Major Martin L. Fracker explained:

> British studies [of combat motivation in World War II] found that repeated air attacks, which became increasingly frightening even though they did little

real damage, seemed to sensitize soldiers to the shock effect. On the other hand, American studies indicated just the opposite: repeated attacks seemed to desensitize soldiers. ... Psychologist Steven Reiss notes that repeated exposure to a fearful stimulus can be either sensitizing or desensitizing, depending upon the exposure condition. Similarly, clinical psychologist Zahava Solomon's research among Israeli soldiers indicates that sensitization occurs with some soldiers while desensitization occurs with others.

This is great news for you, the writer, if not great news for soldiers in battle. It means that the psychological reality of a particular moment of high drama is up to you: You can have your character cringe or refuse to flinch, as both are psychologically possible.

Did You Know?

Not only will different people react differently to moments of high drama, but the same person will display different behaviors in situations that are not so different one from another. Your character may wait patiently in one set of circumstances and pace anxiously in another. Confronted by one moment of high drama, say, a raging fire in broad daylight, your character may act heroically, but confronted by a slightly different moment of high drama, say, a raging fire in the middle of the night, she may completely lose her composure. What makes one situation different enough from another situation to elicit radically different reactions? No one can say for sure.

For example, the average Brit was demoralized by the German bombings in World War I and not demoralized by the German bombings in World War II, because an array of circumstances were different. If you set up a dramatic scene like an aerial bombardment one way, your characters are likely not to budge. If you set it up differently, the same characters are likely to flee. The characters haven't changed—only their circumstances have.

Food for Thought

• How emotionally prepared is your character to weather a moment of high drama?

• What high dramas has your character already experienced in life?

• What sort of high drama would your character be most prepared and least prepared to handle?

SCENARIO NO. 21

LATE AT NIGHT

It is three in the morning and your character can't sleep. Consider what might be keeping your character awake. A guilty conscience? An upcoming confrontation with a competitor? Impending news about medical test results? Creative thoughts? General stress? Excitement about a love relationship? What is likely to be keeping your character awake at three in the morning?

Get a detailed picture in mind of your character at three in the morning, up and out of bed, finding himself unable to sleep. Is the house completely quiet, or can your character hear the refrigerator rumbling and the bedside clock ticking? How many lights does he turn on? What is he wearing? When you have a detailed picture in mind, proceed to the following questions.

1. How does your character react to finding himself wide awake at three in the morning?

   A) Fearfully?
   B) Anxiously?
   C) Wryly?

D) Angrily?

E) Philosophically?

• •

A) Reacting fearfully is consistent with a weak, perhaps disturbed character who regularly regresses to a childhood state of fear, is afraid of the noises he hears and of what might be lurking in the shadows, and who likely has a history of childhood trauma and abandonment issues.

B) Reacting anxiously is consistent with a character who finds himself under a lot of stress, has been awakened because of some specific worry or worries, and will spend the next hour or two wide awake and panicked about how he can possibly handle his current problems.

C) Reacting wryly is consistent with an intelligent, educated, ironic character of the professional class, a world-weary lawyer or a professor of literature, who is amused by the antics of human beings, including finding themselves wide awake at three in the morning.

D) Reacting angrily is consistent with a narcissistic character who believes that he is entitled to an uninterrupted night's sleep, perfect service in restaurants, sunshine when he vacations, and gold bathroom fixtures.

E) Reacting philosophically is consistent with a secure, worldly character who has learned not to turn minor irritations into catastrophes and who, in the morning, will not even remember that his night's sleep had been briefly interrupted.

How does your character react to finding himself wide awake at three in the morning?

2. Assume that it makes your character anxious to find himself wide awake at three in the morning. What does he do to manage that anxiety?

A) Drink hot milk?

B) Drink Scotch?

C) Pace?

D) Surf the Internet?

E) Go for a drive?

• •

A) Drinking hot milk is consistent with a mild-mannered character who prefers quiet to drama, is reclusive by nature, and whose anxiety may run deeper than anyone imagines, himself especially.

B) Drinking Scotch is consistent with a tough, hard-boiled character who relishes his self-image as a worldly, no-nonsense kind of person and who likes rugged pursuits and the occasional rough sex.

C) Pacing is consistent with a brooding character who is troubled by his own nature, by the foibles and weaknesses of human nature, and by existential questions about the meaning of life.

D) Surfing the Internet is consistent with a character who keeps anxiety at bay by darting from one enthusiasm to the next, one piece of information to the next, and one Web site to the next.

E) Going for a drive is consistent with a character who loves jazz, film noir, the solitude of the road, and the theme music and visual effects of *Taxi Driver*.

What does your character do to reduce his anxiety about being wide awake in the middle of the night?

3. Your character hears a car alarm go off outside his window. What does your character do?

    A) Go outside to investigate?
    B) Go to the window and look out?
    C) Go to the window and peek out?
    D) Wait for the alarm to stop and then go to the window?
    E) Nothing?

A) Going outside to investigate is consistent with a confident, courageous character who doesn't think twice about walking into harm's way and who considers himself tough and self-reliant.

B) Going to the window and looking out is consistent with a sensible character who responds appropriately in difficult situations and neither takes outlandish risks nor backs away from danger.

c) Going to the window and peeking out is consistent with a reclusive, timid character who hides behind curtains and leads a shadowy, secretive life edged by paranoia.

D) Waiting for the alarm to stop and then going to the window is consistent with an anxious character who deals with his anxiety by avoiding tense situations and, as a consequence, missing out on love and adventure.

E) Doing nothing is consistent with a bored, perhaps depressed character who takes little interest in the doings of the world, doesn't feel community-minded, and wouldn't care if a neighbor's car got stolen—or if his own did, for that matter.

What would your character do if, at three in the morning, a car alarm went off outside?

4. Your character has been up for two hours. What does he do?

   A) Still try to get in an hour's worth of sleep?
   B) Shower and get ready for the new day?
   c) Think about taking the day off?
   D) Call someone in a later time zone?
   E) Throw on some clothes and go out for breakfast?

A) Still trying to get in an hour's worth of sleep is consistent with a character who prizes routine and who feels disoriented, and even lost, when his routine is interrupted.

B) Showering and getting ready for the new day is consistent with a flexible, even-tempered character who is able to adjust on the fly to changed circumstances and who prides himself on making the best of a bad situation.

c) Thinking about taking the day off is consistent with a dramatic, grandiose character who dislikes routine work and who uses the least excuse to skip out and play hooky.

D) Calling someone in a later time zone is consistent with a character who is responsible enough not to wake someone in the middle of the night for no good reason but needy enough to feel compelled to solicit a friendly ear.

E) Throwing on some clothes and going out for breakfast is consistent with a restless, agitated character who feels itchy in his own skin and who takes comfort in mingling with other misfits breakfasting in the middle of the night.

What would your character do if he were still awake at five in the morning?

5. If your character began waking up in the middle of the night on a regular basis, how likely is it that he would resort to prescription medication to deal with the problem?

    A) Entirely likely?
    B) Quite likely?
    C) Fifty-fifty chance?
    D) Quite unlikely?
    E) Completely unlikely?

A) Being entirely likely to resort to sleep medication is consistent with a character with addictive tendencies who has probably run the gamut from situational abuse to dependence with at least one drug.

B) Being quite likely to resort to sleep medication is consistent with a conventional character who believes in the efficacy of pharmaceuticals and who turns to prescription medications at the first sign of a cough, itch, or worry.

C) Possessing a fifty-fifty chance of resorting to sleep medication is consistent with a relatively independent-minded character who would prefer to solve his emotional problems without resorting to drugs but who has been known to self-medicate.

D) Being quite unlikely to resort to sleep medication is consistent with a fully independent-minded, autonomous character who understands that drugs have their place but who prefers to deal with emotional challenges through self-analysis and personality growth.

E) Being completely unlikely to resort to sleep medication is consistent with a stubborn character who takes pride in never asking for help and never accepting help of any sort, including pharmaceutical help.

How likely is your character to resort to sleep medication?

6. Your character remained awake for an hour and then was able to get back to sleep. In the morning, does your character:

    A) Complain loudly about his bad night's sleep?

    B) Worry that terrible sleep problems are beginning?

    C) Worry that he will be too tired to have a productive day?

    D) Smile wryly at his episode of mild insomnia?

    E) Not give it a thought?

A) Complaining loudly about his bad night's sleep is consistent with a character who likes to whine, dramatize his difficulties, and show little empathy or concern for the difficulties of others, many of which are far worse than his own.

B) Worrying that terrible sleep problems are beginning is consistent with an anxious hypochondriac who reckons on deathbed pneumonia with every cough and fears flesh-eating bacteria on every doorknob.

C) Worrying that he will be too tired to have a productive day is consistent with a character who is inclined to react to situations with negative self-talk and to move gloomily through life.

D) Smiling wryly at his episode of mild insomnia is consistent with an ironic, self-aware character who is able to laugh at life's little difficulties and is constitutionally antagonistic to turning molehills into mountains.

E) Not giving it a thought is consistent with a busy character whose life is so pressure-packed and demanding that there is no room left to contemplate incidental matters, the good ones, unfortunately, as well as the bad.

How does your character react in the morning?

Situations to Consider

What would your character do if:

    • It was a strange noise that awakened him?

    • The electricity went out?

- He lay in bed counting sheep for an hour?
- His mate continued sleeping soundly?
- His mate woke up and asked what was wrong?
- There was a full moon out?
- This was the fifth night in a row that he had come fully awake at three in the morning?

Other Late-at-Night Situations

Put your character in the most appropriate of the following situations and think through how he would act and react. If you like, flesh out the scene by adding one conflict and one surprise.

- sitting alone in a diner at three in the morning
- waiting for a train at three in the morning
- driving a cab at three in the morning
- arriving in a foreign capital at three in the morning
- leaving a bar at three in the morning
- having the phone ring at three in the morning
- ending a swing shift at three in the morning

Sleepwalking

A phenomenon like sleepwalking, which is both striking and seemingly rare, is actually not so rare—and very poorly understood. As defined by Sleep Channel (http://sleepdisorderchannel.net):

> Sleepwalking, or somnambulism, is a common arousal disorder that is especially prevalent among children. ... Although the exact prevalence of sleepwalking in adults is not known, it is estimated to be as high as 10%. ... Currently, there is nonspecific medical evidence that suggests that there may be psychiatric issues involved in sleepwalking and that the actions of sleepwalkers in certain cases may not be autonomous and need to be reevaluated. ... For example, in Britain, a man actually killed someone while sleepwalking. The issue was whether or not to acquit the defendant on the basis of autonomic actions or to find him insane and release him to treatment for mental illness.

Did You Know?

Sleepwalkers are not allowed to serve in the armed services, partly because of the threat they might pose to themselves and to others if, while they were sleepwalking, they accessed their weapon or other dangerous equipment. Imagine for a second that your character (male or female) has been rejected from military duty for some reason. In *your* character's case, what might that reason be?

Food for Thought

• Is your character friendly at three in the morning?

• Does your character have a history of insomnia or other sleep disorders? If so, what do these troubles suggest about his personality?

• How often does your character see the dawn?

SCENARIO NO. 22

SUDDEN LEADERSHIP

Your character is thrust into a sudden leadership role. Depending on the character you're investigating and the nature of the novel you're writing, choose one of the following three sudden leadership roles into which to drop your character.

- Your character is second in command of an infantry company, and his immediate superior is killed.

- Your character is voted jury foreperson at a murder trial.

- After the group's guide falls off a cliff and drowns, your character is the only person left who knows the way out of the mountains.

Choose the scenario that best suits your character and get it clearly in mind. What was your character's mind-set just before this leadership role was thrust upon him? Picture your character learning that he must lead, taking that news in, and then beginning to lead. When you have your scenario clearly in mind, proceed to the following questions.

1. How does your character don the leadership mantle?

   A) With reluctance?

B) With trepidation?
C) With enthusiasm?
D) With bravado?
E) By immediately issuing orders?

A) Donning the leadership mantle with reluctance is consistent with a thoughtful character who may be sure of his capabilities but who also understands that with leadership comes ethical conflicts (for instance, about who should live and who should die).

B) Donning the leadership mantle with trepidation is consistent with an anxious, fearful character who has avoided leadership roles in the past and who may in fact rise to the occasion but whose first reaction is one of fright.

C) Donning the leadership mantle with enthusiasm is consistent with a youthful, reckless, spirited character who looks for challenges, takes pride in his capabilities, and is likely aggressive and optimistic by nature.

D) Donning the leadership mantle with bravado is consistent with a defended character who is much less confident than he appears and who is likely to compensate for that lack of confidence and poor self-image with strictness and harsh discipline.

E) Immediately issuing orders is consistent with a fearless, tough-minded, worldly character who knows that emergencies must be dealt with directly and immediately and that followers must be allowed no doubts about who is in charge.

How does your character don the leadership mantle?

2. Your character isn't sure what to do next. How does he proceed?

A) Asks someone for advice?
B) Sleeps on the matter?
C) Remains indecisive, despite the group's grumblings?
D) Makes a rapid, thoughtful decision?
E) Makes a careless, impulsive decision?

A) Asking someone for advice is consistent with a socialized, conventional character who hasn't been in a position of leadership before and who thinks that consulting is the same as leading.

B) Sleeping on the matter is consistent with a thoughtful character who likes to weigh his options before acting and who is likely to arrive at reasonable solutions—although not necessarily as quickly as circumstances require.

C) Remaining indecisive is consistent with an anxious, passive character who lacks self-confidence and who in the past has tended to make decisions by default, letting things happen to him rather than acting proactively and decisively.

D) Making a rapid, thoughtful decision is consistent with a character who has trained himself to deal with emergencies, as for instance, through martial arts training, medical training, or specialized military or police training.

E) Making a careless, impulsive decision is consistent with an immature, reckless character who tends not to think about the consequences of his actions, likely has addictive tendencies, and is prone to accidents and disasters.

How will your character proceed when he isn't sure what to do next?

3. Someone in the group confronts your character about his latest decision. How does your character react?

    A) Takes a vote?
    B) Bullies the objector into silence?
    C) Ignores the objection?
    D) Holds an open discussion?
    E) Acquiesces and changes his mind?

A) Taking a vote is consistent with a liberal-minded character who hasn't experienced leading in the real world and doesn't realize that even in a democracy voters do not make the hard decisions—they elect others to make those decisions.

B) Bullying the objector into silence is consistent with a mean-spirited, aggressive, and probably abusive character who uses physical and verbal intimidation to silence his opponents.

c) Ignoring the objection is consistent with a passive-aggressive character who may seem agreeable on the surface but who is really furious and stubbornly controlling beneath his placid exterior.

D) Holding an open discussion is consistent with a fair-minded character who is willing not only to hear what people have to say but to actually listen to opposing viewpoints before making his decision.

E) Acquiescing and changing his mind is consistent with a weak, frightened character who is likely to regularly change his mind depending on whom he last talked to—or was confronted by.

What would your character do if someone in the group confronted him about a decision?

4. The group is faced with a serious external threat. Does your character:

    A) Feel too frightened to lead?
    B) Feel quietly calm and equal to the challenge?
    C) Ask to be relieved of his leadership duties?
    D) Rally the group and motivate it to meet the challenge?
    E) Lead the group in retreat?

A) Feeling too frightened to lead is consistent with a character who may do reasonably well when not seriously challenged but whose basic anxiety and lack of self-confidence prevent him from rising to the occasion when the occasion is seriously challenging.

B) Feeling quietly calm and equal to the challenge is consistent with a strong-minded, self-confident, and perhaps fatalistic character who demands of himself that he act honorably and courageously, not flinch, and take full responsibility for leading.

c) Asking to be relieved of his leadership duties is consistent with a superficially self-confident character who maintains a confident façade by dint of will until the stress becomes too great, at which time he resigns, retires, withdraws, or flees the country.

D) Rallying the group and motivating it to meet the challenge is consistent with a character who loves competition, probably engaged in competitive sports or a competitive business, and categorizes all aspects of life in terms of winning and losing.

E) Leading the group in retreat is consistent with a careful, calculating character who understands the place of strategic retreat in life or, alternatively, with a frightened, cowardly character whose basic impulse, even as a leader, is to run.

How does your character react to a serious external threat?

5. Your character must give a hard order. Does he:

    A) Do so immediately and decisively?
    B) Do so immediately and impulsively?
    C) Do so immediately but reluctantly?
    D) Brood about the decision for days?
    E) Delegate someone else to decide?

A) Giving the order immediately and decisively is consistent with a no-nonsense character who understands that good decisions can be made quickly, that waiting is not always prudent or virtuous, and that any decision can result in success or failure—so why not just decide?

B) Giving the order immediately and impulsively is consistent with an immature character who acts before he thinks and often lives to regret the consequences of his actions—if he does live.

C) Giving the order immediately but reluctantly is consistent with a self-confident character who likes to look at many sides of a situation, who would love to act only after obtaining sufficient information to make an informed decision, but who understands that enough information really isn't attainable, as only a clairvoyant can predict the future.

D) Brooding about the decision for days is consistent with an anxious, possibly pampered character who prefers fantasy to reality, is put in a panic by choosing, and probably has regular trouble acting autonomously and independently.

E) Delegating someone else to decide is consistent with a self-protective character who likes to insulate himself from the consequences of actions, constructing a universe where the buck always stops with someone else and never quite makes it to his desk.

What does your character do when confronted by the need to give a hard order?

6. Your character's leadership role ends. Is he:

A) Relieved?
B) Disappointed?
C) Proud?
D) Depressed?
E) Jubilant?

A) Feeling relieved is consistent with an anxious character who has limited emotional resources, who may be able to rise to the occasion but who is stretched to the limit by challenging situations, and who prefers the shadows to the limelight.

B) Feeling disappointed is consistent with a powerful, self-confident character who enjoys challenge, is already eager for the next challenge, and chafes at the bit between challenges.

C) Feeling proud is consistent with a thoughtful, self-contained character who is able to bask in the glow of his accomplishments, take success in stride, and quietly await the next opportunity to shine.

D) Feeling depressed is consistent with a character who has had few opportunities to shine in life, who enjoyed this sudden leadership role, and who is now resigned to returning to his humdrum life—a prospect that brings with it the blues.

E) Feeling jubilant is consistent with a character who, although able to take pride in performing well under duress, experiences great relief when removed from a position of leadership, and prefers peace and quiet to heroism and drama.

How does your character react to his sudden leadership duties ending?

Situations to Consider

What would your character do if:

- The group turned on him?

- He discovered that a member of the group was sabotaging the group's efforts?

- He began to feel unequal to leading?

- He began to feel that someone else in the group would make the better leader?

- He were held responsible after the fact for the group's actions?

- The group suggested that he change his leadership style?

- The group refused to follow?

Other Sudden Leadership Situations

Put your character in the most appropriate of the following situations and think through how he would act and react. If you like, flesh out the scene by adding one conflict and one surprise.

- sent to head a company branch office located in a foreign country
- the only person at a train wreck able to triage the survivors
- family crisis
- building fire
- only uninjured person at an accident site
- advancement at work to a position of real leadership
- organizing a start-up venture

Charisma

Does your character possess that recognizable but indefinable something known as charisma? As you investigate your character, ask yourself not only whether he possesses charisma but if there might be a wellspring of charisma available to your character, some untapped resource or potential. People do sometimes become sexier, more powerful, and more charismatic when the situation presents itself. Might that be true for your character?

Did You Know?

Charisma comes from the Greek *kharisma*, "divine favor," as well as from similar Greek roots, for instance, *kharizesthai*, "to favor." In Christian theology, charisma is an extraordinary power, such as the ability to perform miracles, granted by the Holy Spirit. Is your character a favorite of the gods? In real life, few people are so favored, but in a novel it is common to encounter charismatic characters—often presented so that we can watch them fall from their great height (and sometimes rise up again).

Food for Thought

• Is your character a born leader?

• Do your character's leadership skills match his ambition?

• What is your character's leadership style (authoritarian, laissez-faire, etc.)?

SCENARIO NO. 23

DIAGNOSED WITH AN ILLNESS

Your character has gone in for a routine physical exam and her doctor discovers something troubling, fears the presence of a life-threatening ailment, and orders a round of exams. In this scenario, consider your character's reactions as she awaits the test results, which aren't due for two weeks.

Get the scenario firmly in mind. Picture your character at the hospital, seeing her doctor, being examined, noticing the worried look on the doctor's face, being told that more tests are required, taking those further tests, and leaving the doctor's office and then the hospital. When you have this scenario firmly in mind, consider the following questions.

1. What is your character's first thought upon hearing the news that she may have a life-threatening illness?

    A) "Why me?"
    B) "What will become of those I leave behind?"
    C) "This can't be happening!"
    D) "I knew I had terrible luck!"
    E) "I can beat this!"

A) Thinking "Why me?" is a common reaction consistent with a life-loving, death-fearing character who has never doubted her own mortality but also has never come to grips with her own mortality.

B) Thinking "What will become of those I leave behind?" is consistent with a responsible character who perhaps has devoted her life to others at the expense of realizing her own potential and dreams.

C) Thinking "This can't be happening!" is consistent with a character who finds herself in the first stage of the grieving process, denial, and who is likely to begin to cycle through the five stages—denial, anger, bargaining, depression, and acceptance—as she awaits her diagnosis.

D) Thinking "I knew I had terrible luck!" is consistent with a pessimistic character who has a negative self-image and a history of unfortunate incidents and accidents, and who takes each new crisis to be further proof that she is personally cursed.

E) Thinking "I can beat this!" is consistent with an optimistic character full of naïve trust in the goodness of the universe or, alternatively, with a strong-willed character who is determined to make her own fate and who believes that putting up a fight is the best way to take responsibility for how life turns out.

What is your character's first thought upon hearing that she may have a life-threatening illness?

2. What does your character do directly upon leaving the hospital?

    A) Sit for some time in her car before driving off?
    B) Immediately call a loved one?
    C) Aimlessly drive around?
    D) Drive home and take a nap?
    E) Drive home and resume her usual routine?

A) Sitting for some time in her car is consistent with a thoughtful character in shock and disbelief who is processing the news and working out her next steps, including who she will tell and what she will tell them.

b) Immediately calling a loved one is consistent with an empathic, sensitive character who is used to sharing every manner of news, from the best to the worst, with her intimates and who gains tremendous strength by virtue of having love in her life.

c) Aimlessly driving around is consistent with an anxious character who can't find the emotional wherewithal to return just like that to her tasks, responsibilities, and everyday life, and who may suddenly find herself taking an account of the other problems in her life, like a loveless marriage or her long-deferred dreams.

d) Driving home and taking a nap is consistent with an already-depressed character for whom this blow may turn a background case of the blues into a depression of clinical proportions.

e) Driving home and resuming her usual routine is consistent with a strong-willed, stoic character who has trained herself to put one foot in front of the other, no matter what, or, alternatively, with a terrified character in full denial who has forced this news out of consciousness.

What does your character do directly upon leaving the hospital?

3. On that first day, does your character:

    A) Tell her mate?
    B) Tell her parents?
    C) Tell her best friend?
    D) Tell her children?
    E) Tell no one?

A) Immediately telling her mate is consistent with a character who finds herself in a strong, enduring intimate relationship where partners openly reveal their deepest fears and worries.

B) Immediately telling her parents is consistent with a needy, immature character who has trouble with autonomous action and independent living or, alternatively, with a character who has an unusually frank and friendly relationship with her parents and feels comfortable letting them know when things aren't going well.

c) Immediately telling her best friend is consistent with a character who cherishes friendship, is available for her friends and considers them available to her, and whose most enduring interpersonal relationships may be with her buddies, perhaps to the irritation and dismay of her children and mate.

D) Immediately telling her children is consistent with a character who may divulge too freely and who, in the past, may have inappropriately burdened her children with news about her lovers, ailments, and complexes.

E) Telling no one is consistent with a stoic, self-reliant, and perhaps depressed character who prefers to deal with crises privately and who rarely seeks the comfort and support of others.

On that first day, whom does your character tell?

4. Does your character react to her situation by experiencing:

    A) Nightmares?
    B) Insomnia?
    c) Stomachaches?
    D) Crying jags?
    E) Irritability?

A) Reacting to the situation with nightmares is consistent with a character who has managed to put the matter of her possible illness out of conscious awareness but who can't keep her unconscious mind from playing out her fears and constructing worst-case scenarios.

B) Reacting to the situation with insomnia is consistent with anxious, brooding, thoughtful character who finds herself uncontrollably obsessing about her situation day and night.

c) Reacting to the situation with stomachaches is consistent with a character for whom anxiety manifests in somatic ways and who probably has a history of missing piano recitals and final exams because of stomachaches, headaches, and other quickly appearing and quickly disappearing ailments.

D) Reacting to the situation with crying jags is consistent with an emotionally fragile character who is likely burdened by many stressors in addition to this one and who may find this crisis taking her to the breaking point.

E) Reacting to the situation with irritability is consistent with a harried, hard-working Type A character who finds herself annoyed that she has to take time out of her busy schedule to worry about possible bad news.

How does your character react to her situation?

5. The day of the test results arrives. What is your character experiencing?

    A) Indifference?
    B) High anxiety?
    C) Anger?
    D) Numbness?
    E) Eager anticipation?

A) Reacting with indifference is consistent with a depressed character who has trained herself to react stoically to crises and disappointments or, alternatively, with an anxious character whose primary psychological defense is denial.

B) Reacting with high anxiety is consistent with a character who is anxious by nature and who manifests that anxiety in a wide variety of situations, from flubbed performances to stammered introductions to missed dental appointments.

C) Reacting with anger is consistent with a volatile, strong-willed, skeptical character who, if the diagnosis comes back positive, may demand to be pointed to the latest research so that she can take charge of her treatment planning.

D) Reacting with numbness is consistent with a character who has been through the emotional wringer while waiting for her test results, possibly cycling several times through the stages of the grief process.

E) Reacting with eager anticipation is consistent with an optimistic character who prides herself on her positive attitude and who has trained herself to hope for the best and deal with whatever comes her way.

What is your character feeling on the day that the test results are due?

6. Your character learns that the tests have proven inconclusive and that she must take some additional tests. What is her reaction?

   A) Disbelief?
   B) Numbness?
   C) Anger?
   D) Despair?
   E) Hopefulness?

A) Reacting with disbelief is consistent with an immature, naïve character who is regularly shocked by the most natural occurrences, like repairmen sometimes arriving late, flights sometimes being delayed, and medical tests sometimes proving inconclusive.

B) Reacting with numbness is consistent with a stressed-out, overburdened character who has defensively shut down and who likely will be emotionally and physically unavailable to her loved ones.

C) Reacting with anger is consistent with a short-tempered, abrasive character who typically blames the messenger for the message and who, if the new tests come back positive, will likely be aggressively unwilling to follow medical advice.

D) Reacting with despair is consistent with an already depressed character whose feelings of helplessness and hopelessness increase with each bit of bad news.

E) Reacting with hopefulness is consistent with an optimistic character who finds it valuable to frame news in its most positive light or, alternatively, with a socialized character who's been taught to put on a happy face irrespective of what she is actually feeling.

What is your character's reaction to the news that more tests are needed?

Situations to Consider

What would your character do if:

   • The suspected disease was AIDS?
   • She was religious?

- She had no will prepared?
- She had just lost a loved one?
- The suspected disease was cancer?
- She had young children?
- She had a vacation planned for the next week?

Other Life-Threatening Situations

Put your character in the most appropriate of the following situations and think through how she would act and react. If you like, flesh out the scene by adding one conflict and one surprise.

- caught in a flood
- kidnapped for ransom
- flying in an airplane experiencing severe problems
- caught in an earthquake
- exposed to a biological agent
- trapped on a sinking ship
- caught in a hurricane

Common Reactions to Traumatic News

How do people react to trauma? The following are some common reactions in the days following a trauma:

- anxiety about being alone, being in other frightening situations, or hearing similarly bad news

- being easily startled by loud noises or sudden movements

- physical symptoms such as tense muscles, trembling or shaking, diarrhea or constipation, nausea, headaches, sweating, tiredness

- lack of interest in usual activities, including loss of appetite and loss of interest in sex

- sleep problems, including getting to sleep and waking in the middle of the night

- problems with thinking, concentration, or remembering things

- guilt and self-doubt for not having acted in some other way during the trauma or for irresponsibly not having done something to prevent the trauma

Did You Know?

Not surprisingly, the longer a person has to wait to hear back on test results, the more his or her anxiety grows. Medical reporter Anna Byk explained in "The Waiting Game," published in the *National Review of Medicine* (www.national reviewofmedicine.com):

> The longer a patient has to wait for mammogram results, the more the anxiety grows. It seems to follow that faster results would naturally reduce the stress and get the patient listening to the diagnosis and her treatment options.
>
> That assumption is exactly right, according to a study published in the April 7 issue of the *Journal of the National Cancer Institute*. The U.S. study looked at 8,453 women who'd had false positive mammograms to measure anxiety levels associated with waiting for results. The researchers found that women who received the results of their follow-up mammogram on the same day suffered less anxiety.

If you want your character to experience a great deal of anxiety in a scenario where bad news may be coming, make her have to wait for the news.

Food for Thought

• How would your character deal with the news that she in fact had the life-threatening illness?

• Would your character ever contemplate suicide?

• What does your character believe about an afterlife?

SCENARIO NO. 24
CAUGHT IN A BIG LIE

Your character has told a big lie and gotten caught. The first thing to do is to get the right sort of lie in mind, as lying to an enemy interrogator during wartime is very different from lying to your mate about your extramarital affairs. The first is correct behavior and heroic, the second nothing of the sort. For the sake of this scenario, let's presume your character has told a big lie to cover up a moral lapse or to avoid trouble. From the following three big lies, choose the one that is most plausible with respect to your character's nature and circumstances.

- Your character is not the biological parent of one of his children, though he has always claimed to be, and that child has just learned the truth.

- Your character killed someone years ago in defensible circumstances and lied about what happened, and the police have now learned about the homicide and your character's part in it.

- Your character came up a class short of graduating from college but has always claimed to be a college graduate, and a prospective employer has just learned the truth of the matter.

Choose the big lie that best suits your character and then picture it in detail. Get into your character's experience of having lied about this for all these years, his worry about exposure, his efforts to keep the lie a secret, and his dread of just this moment. Now picture the moment when the lie is exposed and your character is confronted either by his child, the police, or a prospective employer. Set the scene carefully and then proceed to the following questions.

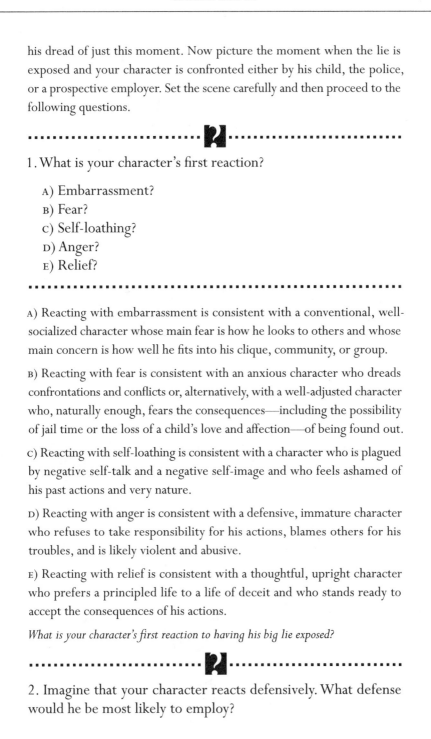

1. What is your character's first reaction?

   A) Embarrassment?
   B) Fear?
   c) Self-loathing?
   D) Anger?
   E) Relief?

A) Reacting with embarrassment is consistent with a conventional, well-socialized character whose main fear is how he looks to others and whose main concern is how well he fits into his clique, community, or group.

B) Reacting with fear is consistent with an anxious character who dreads confrontations and conflicts or, alternatively, with a well-adjusted character who, naturally enough, fears the consequences—including the possibility of jail time or the loss of a child's love and affection—of being found out.

c) Reacting with self-loathing is consistent with a character who is plagued by negative self-talk and a negative self-image and who feels ashamed of his past actions and very nature.

D) Reacting with anger is consistent with a defensive, immature character who refuses to take responsibility for his actions, blames others for his troubles, and is likely violent and abusive.

E) Reacting with relief is consistent with a thoughtful, upright character who prefers a principled life to a life of deceit and who stands ready to accept the consequences of his actions.

What is your character's first reaction to having his big lie exposed?

2. Imagine that your character reacts defensively. What defense would he be most likely to employ?

A) Rationalization (presenting reasons for having maintained the lie)?

B) Denial (refusing to admit the truth of the matter)?

C) Regression (throwing a tantrum like a two-year-old)?

D) Displacement (kicking the nearest object)?

E) Projection (imputing feelings to the other person that are really his own)?

. . . .

A) Employing the defense mechanism known as rationalization is consistent with a logical, intelligent, argumentative character who supposes that if an argument sounds reasonable people will be fooled or seduced into believing it.

B) Employing the defense mechanism known as denial is consistent with a character who has powerful needs to hide the truth from himself and, just as importantly, from others, and is often the defense of choice of the addict and the alcoholic.

C) Employing the defense mechanism known as regression is consistent with a histrionic character who is wound tight and on the verge of falling apart and who emotionally crumbles when his secret is revealed.

D) Employing the defense mechanism known as displacement is consistent with a character who lacks awareness and has no clue that, for example, he is lashing out at his wife because his daughter now knows the truth about her paternity.

E) Employing the defense mechanism known as projection is consistent with a character who sees in others feelings that they do not possess, for example, projecting onto the prospective employer feelings of embarrassment when it is the character who is feeling embarrassed.

What sort of defensive posture, if any, would your character adopt?

. . . .  . . . .

3. Your character is given some time to think about whether or not he would like to fully and honestly explain himself. At the end of that time, what has your character decided? (For the sake of this question, let's presume that it isn't foolish to reveal the truth.

That said, in the homicide scenario, for instance, a sturdy silence might be the most sensible approach.)

A) To apologize and reveal everything?
B) To reveal everything but without an apology?
C) To strategically reveal a few things?
D) To stonewall and reveal nothing?
E) To deny that he ever lied?

••

A) To apologize and reveal everything is consistent with a mature, self-aware, self-confident character who is able to tolerate the truth, even if it reflects poorly on him, and who is capable of apologizing, a feat beyond the psychological capabilities of most people.

B) To reveal everything but without apologizing is consistent with an intellectual, postmodern character who believes that human affairs are so complex that there is no point in apologizing for an action that, as the poison fruit of so many intricate causes and subjective meanings, is really beyond understanding and blame.

C) To strategically reveal a few things is consistent with a savvy, world-wise character who retains control of the information he possesses, is good at keeping secrets, and rarely blurts out anything revealing—or real.

D) To stonewall and reveal nothing is consistent with a character who has trained himself in the art of self-protection and who has the strength of character that complete silence requires as well as the weakness of character that makes a stubborn silence his favorite recourse.

E) To deny that he ever lied is consistent with an aggressive, grandiose character who likely has never taken responsibility for his actions—and never will.

Given some time, how does your character decide to deal with the matter?

4. During the time that your character kept this matter a secret, did he confide in anyone? Did he confide in his:

A) Mate?
B) Best friend?

c) Parent?
D) Therapist?
E) In no one?

• •

A) Confiding in a mate is consistent with a character who sees his relationship as a truly intimate one and who has sufficient confidence in his mate to reveal even the unflattering and sordid details of life without fear of being harshly judged.

B) Confiding in a best friend is consistent with a character who takes friendship seriously, elevates it to something of a sacred principle, and can be expected to be there for his best friends even when they are in the wrong.

c) Confiding in a parent is consistent with a character who has a close, warm, and intimate relationship with his parent or, alternatively, with a dependent character who is immaturely and unnaturally tied to his parent and has been trained to reveal too much and rely too heavily.

D) Confiding in a therapist is consistent with a narcissistic character of the professional class who likes to create a support system of hired help, from masseur to counselor, each of whom is trained to take confessions well.

E) Not confiding in anyone is consistent with a closed, defensive, private character who is guarded and watchful, says little, empathizes poorly, and is vigilant to the point of paranoia.

During the time your character kept this secret, in whom, if anyone, did he confide?

•  •

5. What does your character believe about lying?

   A) People should never lie?
   B) People will occasionally lie, but they should keep their lying to a bare minimum?
   c) There are many occasions when white lies are appropriate?
   D) There are many sorts of lies that need telling, and for a variety of reasons?
   E) It is an absolute necessity to lie, as everyone lies?

• •

A) Believing that people should never lie is consistent with a small-minded, moralistic, hypocritical, probably conservative and religious character who is harsh, critical, and punitive in his dealing with others.

B) Believing that people should keep their lying to a bare minimum is consistent with a conventional character who adheres to society's norms, prefers to fit in rather than to make waves, and is blissfully unconcerned about telling lies to little children, for instance, about the existence of Santa Claus and the Tooth Fairy.

C) Believing that there are many occasions when white lies are appropriate is consistent with a compassionate character who understands that rabid truth-telling is often an excuse for bullying, criticizing, and justifying cruelty.

D) Believing that there are many reasons to lie is consistent with an intelligent character who understands that the "whole truth" is a suspect idea and that personal responsibility demands that he act authentically, which may well mean fabricating and confabulating.

E) Believing that it is an absolute necessity to lie is consistent with an antisocial character filled with hatreds and resentments who sees truth-telling as weakness and everyone he encounters as a fool and potential victim.

What does your character believe about lying?

6. A new opportunity to tell a big lie arises. How has being caught in one big lie affected your character?

    A) He will not lie again?
    B) He is considerably less likely to lie again?
    C) He is slightly less likely to lie again?
    D) He is just as likely to lie again?
    E) He is more likely to lie again, only with the intention of lying better this time?

A) Not lying again is consistent with a strong-willed character for whom lying was never pathological or habitual, who takes pride in manifesting self-control, and who is perhaps a little on the moralistic side.

B) Being considerably less likely to lie again is consistent with a character who is open enough to learn from experience, sufficiently frightened by or uneasy with the consequences of being found out to prefer truthfulness, and more mature as a result of having lived through the lie and its exposure.

C) Being slightly less likely to lie again is consistent with a character who is a slow learner, who tends to repeat his mistakes, and who is attracted to lying as a way out of difficult circumstances.

D) Being just as likely to lie again is consistent with a character who believes that lying is the best response to a difficult situation, who feels no moral sting from lying, and who supposes—cynically or accurately—that everyone lies and that therefore he is entitled to lie as necessary.

E) Being more likely to lie again is consistent with a frightened, devious, well-defended character who has become a pathological liar over time and who now lies about everything, even when telling the truth might serve him better.

Having been caught in one big lie, what are the chances that your character will lie again, should the opportunity or necessity arise?

Situations to Consider

What would your character do if:

- The secret exposed was about his sexual orientation?
- The secret exposed was about an act of cowardice?
- The secret exposed was about a long-deceased family member?
- The secret exposed was about embezzlement?
- The secret exposed was about a girlfriend's abortion?
- The secret exposed was about an addiction?
- The secret exposed was about a love affair?

Other Caught Situations

Put your character in the most appropriate of the following situations and think through how he would act and react. If you like, flesh out the scene by adding one conflict and one surprise.

- caught bringing undeclared items through Customs
- caught pilfering stationery from the office
- caught snacking on grapes while shopping at the supermarket

- caught glancing at sexually explicit material
- caught playing favorites among his children
- caught not working while on company time

Lying Cues

Do you know what cues indicate that a person is lying? According to Sean Henahan in "The Science of Lying," an article from Access Excellence @ The National Health Museum (http://accessexcellence.org):

> [I]nvestigators carefully reviewed videotapes of President Bill Clinton's testimony to the grand jury in which he denied any relationship with the intern Monica Lewinsky, ... [versus] the preliminary section of the president's testimony in which he gave his name ..., along with a tape of a fundraiser before a friendly crowd, as controls ...
>
> The comparison of the president's known truthful and nontruthful answers showed a 100% increase in leaning, a 355% increase in drinking and swallowing ... and a 268% reduction in blinking. When compared with the fundraiser before the friendly audience, there was a 402% increase in the use qualifiers and modifiers, a 1733% increase in speech errors and a 1444% increase in stuttering ...

Want a character to lie and get caught? A few speech errors, a reduction in blinking, an increase in leaning, a little more drinking and swallowing, and voila!

Did You Know?

Why, as the story has it, did Pinocchio's nose grow each time he lied? Maybe because the raising of the hand to the nose has been reported in many cultures as a movement associated with lying. This may be related to the fact that the nose contains erectile tissues that engorge when a person is lying. For this reason, the physical changes associated with mendacity are sometimes called the Pinocchio Effect.

Food for Thought

- What sort of big lie might your character tell?
- How well does your character keep personal secrets?
- How well does your character keep other people's secrets?

SCENARIO NO. 25

DEATH OF A PARENT

In this scenario, your character learns that one of her parents has died. Choose whether the parent dies suddenly or after a long illness, whether it is the mother or the father, and other elements that will allow you to get this scenario clearly in mind. A sudden death is the more dramatic event and may elicit the larger emotions, but its very intensity may obscure what your character is really feeling, so there are investigative pluses and minuses to either choice. If you have the time and the inclination, run through the scenario twice, once imagining a sudden death and once an anticipated death.

Picture your character in the moments before receiving the news. What is she doing? What is she feeling? Hear the phone ringing and picture your character answering it. Who delivers the news? The surviving parent? A sibling? An emergency room nurse? A police officer? Get the details clearly in mind and then proceed to the following questions.

1. Your character learns that a parent has died. What is her first reaction?

   A) Shock and disbelief?
   B) Sadness?

c) Anxiety?

D) Anger?

E) Relief?

. . . .

A) Shock and disbelief are normal, unremarkable reactions. A reaction of extreme shock (for instance, fainting away upon hearing the news) is consistent with a busy character who is good at juggling multiple tasks and for whom, because she is internally and externally so hectic, the news of her parent's death hardly registers in those first few instants—and then registers with a bang.

B) Sadness is a normal, unremarkable reaction. A reaction of extreme sadness (for instance, dissolving into an uncontrollable crying jag) is consistent with a melancholic character who is sad much of the time, expects life to present her with reasons for tears, and quite possibly lives alone in a fantasy world.

c) Anxiety is a normal, unremarkable reaction. A reaction of extreme anxiety (for instance, experiencing heart attack-like symptoms) is consistent with a fearful character with low self-esteem who, confronted by the practical realities of funeral arrangements and the psychological reality of loss, is instantly and severely unnerved.

D) A reaction of anger is consistent with a tumultuous, even aggressive character who reacts to her parent's death as a personal insult and a victory for the universe.

E) A reaction of relief is consistent with a character who has had long-simmering conflicts with her parent or, alternatively, with a character who is happy to see the terrible suffering of her parent finally end.

What is your character's first reaction upon hearing that her parent has died?

2. How does your character relate with her siblings as they gather after the death? Does she:

A) Commiserate?

B) Point fingers?

c) Console?

D) Discuss arrangements?

E) Keep her distance?

. . . .

A) Commiserating is consistent with a character in a dramatic family where wailing and hand-wringing are the norm, expressiveness is valued, and every feeling is deeply felt.

B) Pointing fingers is consistent with a character who is part of an acrimonious, conflict-filled family who take every opportunity—even, and perhaps especially, the death of a parent—to bicker.

C) Consoling is consistent with a character who is part of a close, loving family where family members notice which family member is hardest hit by an event and gather around that person to offer love and support.

D) Discussing arrangements is consistent with a character who is part of a matter-of-fact, unemotional family who pride themselves on their calmness and correctness or, alternatively, with a character who masks her emotional pain by keeping up appearances and who is likely to eventually buckle.

E) Keeping her distance is consistent with a character who is part of a family whose members are estranged from one another, resentful of one another, and whose interactions are cursory and polite or, alternatively, with a despondent character who is pulling away from others out of grief and sadness.

How does your character relate to her siblings as they gather?

. . . .  . . . .

3. What is your character feeling about her surviving parent?

A) Anxiety?

B) Anger?

C) Compassion?

D) Closeness?

E) Estrangement?

. . . .

A) Feeling anxiety about her surviving parent is consistent with an educated, psychologically minded character who knows that a surviving spouse is likely to suffer a major physical illness, even a life-threatening one, in the months after a mate's death.

B) Feeling anger toward her surviving parent is consistent with a character who has chosen sides between her parents, loved her deceased parent more than her surviving parent, and blames the surviving parent for causing the death—perhaps by a lifetime of hounding or abuse.

C) Feeling compassion for her surviving parent is consistent with an empathic character who may or may not love her parent deeply but who understands and appreciates his pain and grief.

D) Feeling close to her surviving parent is consistent with a character who loves her surviving parent, shares in that parent's sadness and sense of loss, and makes herself available as a shoulder to lean on.

E) Feeling estranged from her surviving parent is consistent with a character who has a life apart from, and probably at some great distance from, her parents and who has returned only out of a sense of duty.

What is your character feeling about her surviving parent?

4. At the funeral, does your character:

    A) Feel intensely more affected than other people present, including other family members?
    B) Feel about as affected as other people present?
    C) Feel considerably less affected than other people present?
    D) Feel like an observer at a stranger's funeral?
    E) Feel like a murderer?

A) Feeling intensely more affected than one's own siblings and other close relatives is consistent with a hypersensitive character who is timid and anxious by nature, lacks self-awareness, and employs her display of emotion to demonstrate that she loved the deceased parent more than anyone else did.

B) Feeling about as affected as others at the funeral is a normal, unremarkable reaction. It is also consistent with a socialized character who feels compelled to fit in, conform to society's rules and roles, and feels embarrassed by either too great or too small a display of emotion in social situations.

c) Feeling considerably less affected is consistent with a character who is reserved by nature, takes pride in not showing her emotions, and actually doesn't feel much emotion even in the face of great loss and tragedy.

d) Feeling like an observer is consistent with an arch, intelligent, modern character whose stance in life, even when she is actively participating, is one of distance and separation.

e) Feeling like a murderer is consistent with a guilt-racked character who habitually takes the blame for events, some of which are fully her responsibility, some of which are marginally her responsibility, and many of which are not her responsibility at all.

How does your character feel at the funeral?

5. The family is dividing up the parent's personal property. What is your character's position?

    A) Wants as many of her parent's possessions as possible?
    B) Passionately wants several items that have sentimental value?
    C) Passionately wants a few items that have sentimental value?
    D) Is indifferent but feels obliged to take a few things?
    E) Wants nothing and takes nothing?

A) Wanting as many items as possible is consistent with a needy, immature, emotionally fragile character whose apparent greediness is actually the attempt to fill up the aching hole in her psyche with material possessions.

B) Passionately wanting several items is consistent with a character who was devoted to her parent and who would take as many mementoes as possible if only that didn't make her appear too greedy.

C) Passionately wanting a few items is consistent with a self-aware character who is modest and unassuming by nature, and knows she will remember her parent primarily through inner recollection—with a few choice items to help.

D) Feeling indifferent but taking a few things out of a sense of obligation is consistent with a character who has long separated from her parent, emotionally as well as physically, and whose contact has likely been grudging and minimal for a long time already.

E) Wanting nothing and taking nothing is consistent with a character who has engaged in a long-standing feud with her parent, perhaps because of physical or emotional abuse in childhood or a traumatic rift in adolescence.

What is your character's position with respect to her parent's personal possessions?

6. What does your character feel on the first anniversary of her parent's death?

    A) Intense sadness?
    B) Anger?
    c) Mild melancholy?
    D) Depression?
    E) Nothing?

A) Feeling intense sadness is consistent with a character who is carrying emotional wounds from childhood and who has those wounds reopened periodically throughout the year on her birthday, during the holiday season, and on the anniversary of her parent's death.

B) Feeling anger is consistent with a character who continues to bear a grudge against the deceased parent and harbors the wish that the parent were still alive so she could give him one last piece of her mind.

c) Feeling mild melancholy is consistent with a secure, self-confident character who knows that death is a natural, inevitable feature of life and who is as easy with that understanding as a person can be—that is, only imperfectly easy.

D) Feeling depressed is consistent with a character who loved her parent, misses that parent, and has her mild, everyday background depression intensified on the anniversary of that loss.

E) Feeling nothing is consistent with a character who has long divorced herself emotionally and physically from her parent and who is experiencing neither loss nor grief.

What does your character feel on the first anniversary of her parent's death?

Situations to Consider

What would your character do if:

- She accidentally caused the death of her parent?
- One parent died and the second parent committed suicide out of grief?
- Her parent's estate was contested by a sibling?
- Her parent's estate was contested by a stranger?
- The parent was an adoptive parent?
- The parent was a stepparent?
- Your character was estranged from the parent?

Other Significant Deaths and Crisis Situations

Put your character in the most appropriate of the following situations and think through how she would act and react. If you like, flesh out the scene by adding one conflict and one surprise.

- the death of an older sibling
- the death of a younger sibling
- the death of her grown child
- the death of her young child
- the death of her mate
- a parent, child, or mate living in a vegetative state after an accident
- a parent, child, or mate vanishing without a trace

After a Parent Dies

According to "Grief Reactions Associated With the Loss of a Parent," released by the National Association for Grief and Loss (http://grieflink. asn.au/parent.html), the following are some common experiences after the death of a parent:

- You may have feelings of sadness, anger, fear, numbness, loneliness, guilt, and confusion.

- Like others before you, you may feel like an orphan—all alone in the world—especially when both parents have died.

- You may suddenly realize that now you are the older generation and that there is no longer a parent to consult, or someone to be there for you in the tough times.

- With the death of the second parent, the opportunity to find out more about your personal and family history is lost, too, and this may cause you further distress.

Did You Know?

Customs vary the world over as to how deaths are mourned and celebrated. Take the *wake*, for instance. The *wake* is so-called because when coffins were dug up in medieval England, a great many were found to have scratches on the inside of the lids. It seemed as if the person inside had been buried alive and had tried to claw her way out. As a result of this observation, people began to sit with the corpse for the twenty-four hours after death just in case the corpse awoke.

Food for Thought

- What is your character's fundamental belief about death? Is it the absolute end of a person or something else?

- What religious and cultural beliefs about death were your character exposed to as a child, and which of them does she still believe?

- Which important people in your character's life have died?

SCENARIO NO. 26

MEETING THE PRESIDENT

Imagine your character is slated for a personal meeting with the president of the United States. First, under what circumstances might this occur? Perhaps your character has done something heroic and is being honored at the White House. Perhaps your character has accomplished something important in his field. If you like, make the rationale for the meeting fanciful or envision a scenario where your character (and you) have no idea why he has been summoned to the White House.

Once you've decided on the reason for this visit, picture your character getting the invitation, thinking about the invitation, preparing himself to go off to Washington, arriving in Washington, and checking into a hotel. Will he arrive at the White House by limo, by rented car, by government car, by cab, or on foot? When you have the scenario clearly in mind, proceed to the following questions.

1. If your character belongs to the same political party as the president, how does he react to the thought of meeting the president?

   A) With awe?
   B) With delight?

c) With trepidation?
d) With anger?
e) With indifference?

....

A) Reacting with awe is consistent with a conventional, naïve, wide-eyed character who is likely to follow rules and customs, obey authority, and become upset with those who defy authority.

B) Reacting with delight is consistent with a happy-go-lucky, optimistic, adventure-seeking character who relishes new experiences and can't wait to explore the White House.

c) Reacting with trepidation is consistent with an anxious character whose anxiety increases in the presence of power and who can be expected to stammer, shake, and grow confused in the Oval Office.

D) Reacting with anger is consistent with a tough-minded, assertive character who is regularly disappointed with politicians, including those in his own party, and who is perhaps gearing up to give the president a piece of his mind—or at least a dirty look.

E) Reacting with indifference is consistent with an intelligent, educated, modern character who suspects that power brokers, especially presidents, are quite ordinary people and deserve little celebration—or even respect.

How does your character react to the thought of meeting a president who is of the same political party as him?

....

2. If your character belongs to a different political party from the president, how does he react to the thought of meeting the president?

A) With anger?
B) With anxiety?
c) With curiosity and respect?
D) With glee?
E) With indifference?

....

A) Reacting with anger is consistent with an assertive, opinionated character who is quick to condemn people and who divides the world into "us" and "them," all of "them" being the enemy.

B) Reacting with anxiety is consistent with a fearful character who feels powerless in general and who predicts that he will feel even more powerless in the presence of a president whose beliefs differ so radically from his own.

C) Reacting with curiosity and respect is consistent with an open-minded, optimistic character who takes pride in withholding judgment about people until he has had the chance to meet them and who genuinely relishes new learning experiences.

D) Reacting with glee is consistent with an ironic, strong-minded character who enjoys telling truth to power and who may even go so far as to openly chastise and berate the president about his policies and attitudes.

E) Reacting with indifference is consistent with an intelligent, cynical, apolitical character whose basic attitude is "a pox on both your houses" and who holds all political parties and all politicians in equal contempt.

How does your character react to the thought of meeting a president who is of a different political party from him?

3. Who does your character tell about the impending meeting?

    A) Everyone?
    B) Friends?
    C) Only close friends and intimates?
    D) Only his mate or best friend?
    E) No one?

A) Telling everyone is consistent with a boisterous, exuberant character who likes to brag, has trouble keeping secrets, and is easily impressed by power, money, and success.

B) Telling his friends is consistent with a sociable character with an extroverted nature who likely travels in a pack, takes group vacations, and is always ready for a party or group gathering.

c) Telling only close friends and intimates is consistent with a conventional character who only shares information within his circle and is likely quite conscious of class and social distinctions.

D) Telling only his mate or best friend is consistent with a careful, quiet character who is open enough to let others in but private and protected enough to keep information, even about a presidential meeting, close to the vest.

E) Telling no one is consistent with a closed, perhaps paranoid character who shuns people, prefers solitude to company, and will likely say very little in his meeting with the president.

Who does your character tell about the impending meeting?

4. The Oval Office meeting takes place. Your character and the president are shaking hands. What is your character feeling?

   A) Excited?
   B) Anxious?
   c) Angry?
   D) Suspicious?
   E) Indifferent?

A) Feeling excited is consistent with a spirited, perhaps youthful and naïve character who is easily thrilled by parades, celebrity weddings, pomp and circumstance, and displays of wealth and power.

B) Feeling anxious is consistent with a fearful character who would prefer to be elsewhere, who experiences life as risk rather than adventure, and who is doubly burdened by his own anxiety symptoms—for instance, by his sweaty palms or upset stomach.

c) Feeling angry is consistent with a belligerent, assertive, opinionated character who is not in awe of power, says what's on his mind, and whose motto is "Damn the consequences!"

D) Feeling suspicious is consistent with a thoughtful, educated character who understands that successful politicians are master manipulators who likely will try to manipulate the person in front of them simply out of force of habit.

E) Feeling indifferent is consistent with an ironic, intelligent, modern character who is amused by the trappings of power, including the way the Oval Office is designed to make visitors feel small, and keenly aware of the great ordinariness of the person with whom he is shaking hands.

What is your character feeling as he shakes hands with the president in the Oval Office?

5. Your character had planned to say something to the president. Does he:

A) Wait for the right moment and speak calmly?
B) Find himself too anxious to speak?
C) Find himself too intimidated to speak?
D) Blurt out the message?
E) Change his mind about speaking?

A) Waiting for the right moment and speaking calmly is consistent with a confident, self-assured, principled character to whom people listen, whose opinions people respect, and who is likely in a leadership position in life.

B) Finding himself too anxious to speak is consistent with a fearful, conventional, socialized character who may intellectually understand that he has the right to speak up but who viscerally experiences the moment as too dangerous to take that risk.

C) Finding himself too intimidated to speak is consistent with a character troubled by issues of low self-esteem and feelings of powerlessness who is likely also burdened by a history of trauma, for instance, growing up in a verbally or physically abusive household.

D) Blurting the message out is consistent with an impulsive, perhaps youthful character who lacks sufficient self-awareness and life experience to know how to inhabit and seize a moment to best effect.

E) Changing his mind about speaking is consistent with an intelligent, thoughtful character who is plagued by his ability to see both sides of a matter, including the potential positive and negative consequences of speaking in this situation.

What does your character do with the message he was planning to deliver?

6. The president asks your character for a special favor. What is your character's first reaction (even before hearing what the favor is)?

A) Curiosity?
B) Delight?
C) Anxiety?
D) Suspicion?
E) Indifference?

A) Reacting with curiosity is consistent with an open, optimistic, life-loving character whose natural reserve and suspiciousness are muted in the moment by a desire to see what the president is about to ask.

B) Reacting with delight is consistent with a naïve character who is easy to manipulate, thrilled to be on the inside with the power-brokers, and ready to turn himself inside-out in order to please.

C) Reacting anxiously is consistent with a nervous, timid character who instantly worries about the consequences of refusing to do the favor and the consequences of agreeing to do the favor, leaving him feeling trapped in a lose-lose situation.

D) Reacting suspiciously is consistent with a world-wise character with lots of life experience who knows that there are few free lunches, good deeds that go unpunished, or special favors that don't come with strings and costs attached.

E) Reacting indifferently is consistent with a cynical character who finds the very phrase "special favor" manipulative and who is prepared to say no irrespective of how seemingly interesting the special favor seems or how persuasively the president argues his case.

How would your character react if the president asked him for a special favor?

Situations to Consider

What would your character do if:

- The meeting was postponed and he was asked to stay in Washington another few days?
- He discovered that the meeting would be with a presidential aide?
- The president turned out to be surprisingly cordial?
- The president turned out to be surprisingly intelligent?
- The president turned out to be surprisingly hostile?
- The president threatened him?
- The president asked him back for a second visit?

Other In-the-Throne-Rooms-of-Power Situations

Put your character in the most appropriate of the following situations and think through how he would act and react. If you like, flesh out the scene by adding one conflict and one surprise.

- arrested at a protest
- attending an A-list party
- meeting the world's richest man
- undergoing an IRS audit
- summoned to a judge's chambers
- questioned by the FBI
- pulled aside at a border crossing

Obedience and Authority

As a rule, people are amazingly obedient in the face of authority. This fact was much more poorly understood before psychologist Stanley Milgram ran his now-famous social-psychological experiments. In those experiments, a volunteer subject serving as a "teacher" in a "learning experiment" was ordered by a researcher in a white coat to shock a "student" whenever the student answered incorrectly. In reality, the "students" were confederates of the experimenter and weren't really being shocked at all; the actual goal of the experiment was to see if people would harm others at the command of a perceived authority figure.

As the shocking (which wasn't actually occurring) continued, the subject would scream, beg to have the experiment stopped, and even feign a heart attack. Did most subjects stop? No! All the experimenter had to do was firmly ask the teachers to continue, and they continued. Milgram explained in *Obedience to Authority: An Experimental View*:

> Before the experiments, I sought predictions about the outcome from various kinds of people. With remarkable similarity, they predicted that virtually all the subjects [the teachers] would refuse to obey the experimenter. The psychiatrists, specifically, predicted that most subjects would not go beyond 150 volts, when the victim makes his first explicit demand to be freed. They expected that only 4 percent would reach 300 volts, and that only a pathological fringe of about one in a thousand would administer the highest shock on the board.
>
> These predictions were unequivocally wrong. Of the forty subjects in the first experiment, twenty-five obeyed the orders of the experimenter to the end, punishing the victim until they reached the most potent shock available on the generator. After 450 volts were administered three times, the experimenter called a halt to the session. Many obedient subjects then heaved sighs of relief, mopped their brows, rubbed their fingers over their eyes, or nervously fumbled cigarettes. Others displayed only minimal signs of tension from beginning to end.
>
> As we moved from the pilot studies to the regular experimental series, people drawn from every stratum of New Haven life came to be employed in the experiment. The experimental outcome was the same as we had observed among the students. Moreover, when the experiments were repeated in Princeton, Munich, Rome, South Africa, and Australia, the level of obedience was invariably somewhat higher than found in the investigation reported in this article. Thus one scientist in Munich found 85 percent of his subjects obedient.

Did You Know?

How different would your character act if he suspected that his conversation with the president was being bugged? Franklin D. Roosevelt, Harry S. Truman, Dwight D. Eisenhower, John F. Kennedy, Lyndon B. Johnson, and Richard M. Nixon all had the Oval Office bugged (though Truman only bugged it briefly, and Johnson only bugged the phones). Think through what personality aspect might be activated if your character suspected that his conversation was being bugged.

Food for Thought

• What are your character's essential feelings about people who wield power?

• What are your character's essential feelings about people who possess enormous wealth?

• What are your character's essential feelings about people who possess celebrity status?

SCENARIO NO. 27
LOVERS' SPAT

Your character and her lover are having a spat about a seemingly trivial matter that nevertheless is provoking a lot of animosity. It might be a spat about
someone coming home late without having called to explain the tardiness,
someone not attending to an errand that he was supposed to handle, someone inviting company over without asking the other, etc. What apparently
inconsequential matter might embroil your character in a lovers' quarrel?

Get your character and her lover clearly in mind and set the stage for
the fight. What does their apartment or house look like? What are they
wearing? Once you have a clear picture of this quarrel, proceed to the
following questions.

1. How often is your character the one to initiate quarrels in this
relationship?

    A) Almost always?
    B) Regularly?
    C) About half the time?
    D) Not very often?
    E) Almost never?

A) Almost always initiating the quarrel is consistent with a bullying character who lacks self-awareness and impulse control, likes to demean and belittle others, and is generally disloyal and untrustworthy.

B) Regularly initiating the quarrel is consistent with a needy, high maintenance, critical character whose insecurities and low self-esteem play themselves out as bickering, quarreling, and a need for drama and attention.

C) Initiating the quarrel about half the time is consistent with a character in a tense, dramatic relationship where both partners keep the flames of disagreement fanned at all times and give as good as they get.

D) Not very often initiating the quarrel is consistent with a character who is distanced from the relationship and so little involved, both emotionally and physically, as to not bother quarreling or, alternatively, with a calm, confident character who doesn't feel compelled to act out when small things go wrong.

E) Never initiating the quarrel is consistent with a passive, perhaps defeated character who feels powerless to get what she wants and needs or, alternatively, with a solid, secure character who eschews quarreling in favor of more reasoned—and effective—ways of communicating.

How often is your character the one to initiate a quarrel?

2. How does your character like to fight?

    A) With logic?
    B) With insults?
    C) With threats?
    D) With histrionics?
    E) By bringing up the past?

A) Employing logic is consistent with an intelligent, educated, passive-aggressive character who masks her underlying coldness and hostility with a veneer of logical argumentation.

B) Employing insults is consistent with an emotionally abusive character who likely was herself verbally abused during childhood and who lashes out with disproportionate ferocity when her opinions are disputed or her desires thwarted.

c) Employing threats is consistent with a physically abusive character who, metaphorically speaking, always has her hand raised to deliver a blow and whose predominant interpersonal style is bullying.

D) Employing histrionics is consistent with an emotionally volatile character with hysterical edge who is driven to turn small problems into earthquakes and who can't ever get satisfied.

E) Employing the past is consistent with a character who stores up grudges and prides herself on remembering everything about the past, although many of those memories turn out to be inaccurate and self-serving.

How does your character like to fight?

3. What would upset your character the most?

    A) Being told she was stupid?
    B) Being told she was a coward?
    c) Being told she was unattractive?
    D) Being told she was selfish?
    E) Being told she was a failure?

A) If being told she was stupid would upset her the most, that is consistent with a character whose self-image is constructed around a felt sense of superior smartness.

B) If being told she was a coward would upset her the most, that is consistent with a character whose self-image is constructed around the idea of machismo.

c) If being told she was unattractive would upset her the most, that is consistent with a character whose self-image is constructed around the need to appear morally, socially, and physically attractive.

D) If being told she was selfish would upset her the most, that is consistent with a character whose self-image is constructed around the idea of service and being there for others.

E) If being told she was a failure would upset her the most, that is consistent with a character whose self-image is constructed around the ideas of winning and losing.

What sort of charge leveled at your character during a squabble would upset your character the most?

4. Who or what does your character blame for provoking most of the squabbles?

   A) Herself?
   B) Her partner?
   C) Both partners equally?
   D) People outside the relationship?
   E) Circumstances and events?

A) Blaming herself is consistent with an anxious character whose low self-esteem and lack of self-worth conspire to produce feelings of self-loathing and guilt.

B) Blaming her partner is consistent with a smug, narcissistic, and grandiose character who feels superior to others, complains that the universe is treating her unfairly, and holds her mate in contempt.

C) Blaming both partners equally is consistent with an even-minded, even-handed, and even-tempered character who possesses sufficient self-awareness to understand her role in the quarrels but insufficient skills and inner resources to end the quarreling.

D) Blaming people outside the relationship is consistent with a beleaguered character who experiences her extended family and her mate's extended family as powerful negative influences.

E) Blaming circumstances and events is consistent with a character who lacks self-awareness, refuses to take responsibility for her actions, and is generally belligerent and opinionated.

Who or what does your character blame for provoking most of the squabbles?

5. Would your character resort to any of the following during a lovers' quarrel?

A) Sarcasm?
B) Name-calling?
C) Threats?
D) Stonewalling?
E) Violence?

A) Resorting to sarcasm is consistent with a weak, ironic, mean-spirited character who imagines that the mockery she employs somehow masks or minimizes her feelings of hostility.

B) Resorting to name-calling is consistent with an immature, impulsive, self-centered character who likely grew up in an environment where name-calling was standard procedure.

C) Resorting to threats is consistent with an aggressive, bullying character whose need to wield power and exert control play out as dramatic utterances of the "I'm walking out the door!" or "I'll cut you off without a penny!" variety.

D) Resorting to stonewalling is consistent with a secretive, solitary character who takes pride in her stoic strength and who more fears the consequences of acid speaking than of stony silence.

E) Resorting to violence is consistent with an antisocial character with addictive tendencies who lacks empathy and compassion, and who was likely vilified and abused as a child.

What would your character resort to during a lovers' quarrel?

6. How often is your character the one to stop fighting first?

A) Always?
B) A good deal of the time?
C) About half the time?
D) Not very often?
E) Never?

A) Always being the one to stop the fighting is consistent with an anxious character who finds conflict impossible to tolerate and who prefers peace to warfare, even if the peace comes at the cost of surrender and a loss of self-esteem.

B) Being the one to stop the fighting a good deal of the time is consistent with a prudent, even-tempered, conciliatory character whose pride is not wounded and whose self-esteem is not diminished by being the first to signal a truce.

c) Being the one to stop the fighting about half the time is consistent with a character who internally keeps score of the balance of power in relationships and who equates a functioning relationship with an even score.

D) Infrequently being the one to stop the fighting is consistent with a stubborn, defended character who ties her self-image to the outcome of squabbles and feels significantly diminished by every perceived loss.

E) Never being the one to stop the fighting is consistent with a rigid, bullying character who is likely prone to drama, troubled by demons and addictions, and guided by the mantra, "Never give in, and never say you're sorry!"

How often is your character the one to stop the fighting?

Situations to Consider

What would your character do if:

- Your character realized she was wrong?
- The fighting escalated beyond its usual limits?
- Her partner threatened to leave?
- Her partner asked her to leave?
- Children came into the room?
- The squabble continued the next day?
- Her partner asked for a divorce?

Other Intimacy Squabble Situations

Put your character in the most appropriate of the following situations and think through how she would act and react. If you like, flesh out the scene by adding one conflict and one surprise.

- a squabble about money
- a squabble about child-rearing practices
- a squabble about religion
- a squabble about an addiction

- a squabble about where to spend a vacation
- a squabble about a career move involving relocation
- a squabble over jealousy

To Fight or to Wait?

In an intimate relationship, does your character explode when she's angry, fight fair, wait until she's calmed down before speaking her mind, or keep her feelings bottled up? Of these four choices, clinicians favor two of them as the healthiest approaches, but opinion is divided about which of these two is more healthy: fighting fair in the heat of the moment or waiting to calm down.

Psychologist Clayton Tucker-Ladd explained in *Psychological Self-Help*:

> There are different professional opinions (and, as yet, little scientific evidence) about how to handle one's anger towards a spouse. Some therapists are against fighting and say to wait until you have cooled down, then discuss it calmly and ask the partner for help with the problem. Others say that all couples should fight, only fight fairly. Bach and Wyden in *The Intimate Enemy* say that fair fighting opens lines of communication, lets us blow off steam, helps us know ourselves, lets us be our real (sometimes angry) selves, leads to greater security because we know what is really going on in the relationship, enables us to change things (have equal power) in the relationship, and produces a more alive, honest and intimate love relationship.

Imagine your character taking a fair fighting workshop. How would she react? At the end of the day, would she be changed in any way?

Did You Know?

In an article titled "Fighting the Fair Way" (http://ub-counseling.buffalo.edu/fighting.shtml), the Counseling Services Office of the State University of New York at Buffalo outlined a five-step fair fighting process that includes (1) getting ready, (2) initializing, (3) responding, (4) negotiating, and (5) ending. Here are the first two steps.

Getting Ready

Deal with small but significant issues when they happen, and know what you're fighting about. Be specific, limited, and direct with your complaint.

<u>UNFAIR</u>
- avoiding or ignoring an issue your partner feels is important
- giving the silent treatment
- gunny sacking—saving up little hurts and hostilities then dumping them on your partner all at once

Initiating

Report your anger appropriately using "I" statements, and deal with your partner's behavior, not his or her personality.

<u>UNFAIR</u>
- generalizing—"You never ..." or "I'm always ..."
- labeling, name calling, character assassination ("You bastard!")
- mind reading—telling partner what he or she is thinking and feeling

Food for Thought

- How likely or unlikely is it for your character to find herself in a long-term intimate relationship?

- In intimate relationships, does your character itch to fight or prefer peace?

- How much fighting in a relationship can your character tolerate: a great deal, a modest amount, or very little?

SCENARIO NO. 28

SUDDEN SUCCESS

Your character has a sudden enormous success. Maybe he wins the lottery. Maybe his widget revolutionizes technology. Maybe he wins a $5,000,000 poker tournament that he entered on a whim. Maybe his novel is mentioned on a celebrity talk show and becomes an instant bestseller. What sort of sudden success might your character experience—and how would it affect him?

Choose a sudden success appropriate to your character's situation: a great victory if he is a warrior, breaking the decade's most important case if he is a detective, and so on. Get the scenario clearly in mind: What was your character doing and thinking before the sudden success hit, how does he learn about the success, is he alone or among others when he hears, etc. When you have the scenario clearly in mind, proceed to the following questions.

1. How does your character find himself reacting to this sudden success?

   A) Cautiously?
   B) Anxiously?
   C) Wryly?

D) Enthusiastically?

E) Philosophically?

• •

A) Reacting cautiously is consistent with a modest, hard-working character who is in the habit of weighing the pros and cons of situations and who anticipates that this success may well come with a shadow side.

B) Reacting anxiously is consistent with a character who finds everything unexpected and abnormally nerve-racking and who is particularly chary of the attention this success will garner him.

C) Reacting wryly is consistent with an ironic, educated character who understands the often arbitrary and whimsical nature of success and who seriously doubts that sudden success brings with it happiness or contentment.

D) Reacting enthusiastically is consistent with a spirited, adventurous, perhaps reckless and ambitious character who sees the world as his oyster and who may gamble, live large, and lavish extravagant gifts on family and friends.

E) Reacting philosophically is consistent with a phlegmatic character of the professional class who likes to play down his accomplishments and successes, while also perhaps taking secret pride and pleasure in them.

How does your character find himself reacting to this sudden success?

• •

2. Assume that your character reacts cautiously. How is that caution manifested?

A) Does he keep the news of the success to himself?

B) Does he make self-deprecating gestures when people try to congratulate him?

C) Does he double-check and triple-check to make sure that the success is real?

D) Does he complain that something bad will soon befall him?

E) Does he credit others for the success?

• •

A) Keeping the news to himself is consistent with a secretive character who may have grown up in a household where misdemeanors were punished like felonies and survival hinged on your ability to not be found out.

B) Making self-deprecating gestures is consistent with a self-effacing character whose basic modesty prevents him from really owning his success or, alternatively, with a sly character whose self-effacing pose masks great ambition and a gift for deviousness.

c) Double-checking and triple-checking is consistent with a skeptical, anxious character who may remember all too clearly those successes that turned out to be mirages and those windfalls that turned out to be swindles.

D) Complaining that something bad will soon befall him is consistent with a pessimistic, superstitious character who has experienced enough bad luck and unfair treatment to have built a life philosophy on the principle of divine whimsical retribution.

E) Crediting others for the success is consistent with a character who feels most comfortable in the background, who associates notoriety with danger, and whose low self-esteem manifests as a need to praise others.

How is your character's cautious reaction manifested?

3. Assume that your character reacts enthusiastically. What form might that enthusiasm take?

A) Might he go drinking and gambling?
B) Might he lavish gifts on his friends and acquaintances?
c) Might he smile and wear a happy expression?
D) Might he express his enthusiasm as increased libido?
E) Might he become boastful and obnoxious?

A) Going off drinking and gambling is consistent with an impulsive character with addictive tendencies who feels justified in giving in to his addictions as a reward for succeeding and who, the more successes he has, may come ever closer to realizing his potential as an alcoholic and compulsive gambler.

B) Lavishing gifts on his friends and acquaintances is consistent with an expansive, passionate character who genuinely enjoys sharing the wealth, likes to see others surprised and pleased, and moves through life optimistically and energetically.

C) Smiling and wearing a happy expression is consistent with a philosophical, self-assured character who understands that life brings with it a fair measure of pain, and therefore, it is wise, bordering on obligatory, that we consciously smile and be happy when a rare good thing happens.

D) Expressing his enthusiasm as increased libido is consistent with an intense, driven character who uses sexual activity both as a reward for succeeding and as a release valve for an overload of built-up adrenaline-fueled energy.

E) Becoming boastful and obnoxious is consistent with a narcissistic character whose relationships tend to be volatile and short-lived, whose mild paranoia makes him suspicious of everyone around him, and who gauges how he is doing in life by whether he is winning or losing.

What form might your character's enthusiasm take?

4. Your character's sudden success has put him in the limelight, and he is asked for his autograph. How does he react?

    A) Shyly?
    B) Grandly?
    C) Ironically?
    D) Stoically?
    E) Angrily?

A) Reacting shyly is consistent with a passive, self-conscious character who has very little experience with, or taste for, the limelight, who likely experiences performance anxiety at work, and who binds that anxiety by working longer and harder than his peers.

B) Reacting grandly is consistent with an arrogant, grandiose, narcissistic character who takes adulation as his due or, alternatively, with a sly, sarcastic character who is enjoying posing grandly during his two minutes of fame.

c) Reacting ironically is consistent with an intelligent, educated character who understands that celebrity is rarely deserved and that for every movie star giving out autographs, ten thousand cancer researchers, far more deserving of adulation, are toiling away in the shadows.

D) Reacting stoically is consistent with a hard-working, no-nonsense character who would far prefer anonymity and to go about his business but who recognizes that refusing to sign autographs would amount to too high-handed a gesture—and one likely to garner him even more unwanted notoriety.

E) Reacting angrily is consistent with an aggressive, self-centered, perhaps violent character who enjoys acting put upon and who finds in an autograph-seeker the perfect target for his barely suppressed rage.

How does your character react to being asked for his autograph?

5. Your character's sudden success provokes a dream. What is the dream about?

    A) A skyscraper crumbling?
    B) A party to which he is not invited?
    c) An orgy?
    D) Being chased and unable to escape?
    E) Showing up to deliver a speech and discovering he is naked?

A) Dreaming that a skyscraper is crumbling is consistent with a fearful character who suspects that his success, which he may consider undeserved, will be short-lived and will crumble before his eyes, leaving him worse off than before.

B) Dreaming of a party to which he is not invited is consistent with a mildly paranoid character who believes that others will punish him and shun him because of his success and who may believe that the people around him are already throwing him murderous glances and whispering behind his back.

c) Dreaming of an orgy is consistent with a passionate, roving, sex-loving character who sees an orgy as the perfect follow-up to or reward for his sudden success and who may spend a lot of his post-success energy on sexual activity.

D) Dreaming that he is being chased and unable to escape is consistent with an anxious character who has been made nervous by this success and whose inchoate fears likely manifest as physical symptoms such as headaches and stomachaches as well as bad dreams.

E) Dreaming that he has shown up naked to deliver a speech is consistent with a character with low self-esteem and feelings of lack of entitlement who can't believe in his success and who is readying himself to be exposed as an imposter.

What sort of dream might be provoked in your character by his sudden success?

6. It is a month later. Has your character:

   A) Become fundamentally happier?
   B) Become depressed?
   C) Become warier?
   D) Become more generous?
   E) Not changed in any fundamental way?

A) Becoming fundamentally happier is consistent with a secure, self-confident character who long wanted and needed success and who is able to relish his success when it finally arrives.

B) Becoming depressed is consistent with an emotionally fragile character for whom depression was already lurking nearby, and who has discovered that success has not changed his underlying feelings of sadness and despair but has only served to heighten them.

C) Becoming warier is consistent with a mildly paranoid, world-wise character who is more attuned to noticing the downside of success, for instance, the negative changes in some of the people around him, than he is able to relish the upside, which is just as real but which he chooses to ignore.

D) Becoming more generous is consistent with a hard-working character who would have loved to be generous all along but who was hamstrung by circumstance and who now, as a result of his sudden success, is able to act on his long-contained generous impulses.

E) Not changing in any fundamental way is consistent with a philosophical, phlegmatic character who views himself analytically and who, from that dispassionate place, concludes that nothing has fundamentally changed in his life and that therefore he shouldn't act differently.

What is your character like a month later?

Situations to Consider

What would your character do if:

- Someone your character knows becomes suddenly successful?
- Your character's sudden success was abruptly overturned?
- The sudden success was tainted in some way?
- The sudden success caused your character's peers to react with envy and disdain?
- The sudden success brought scam artists out of the woodwork?
- The sudden success was followed by a significant failure?
- The sudden success was followed by an even greater success?

Other Sudden Success Situations

Put your character in the most appropriate of the following situations and think through how he would act and react. If you like, flesh out the scene by adding one conflict and one surprise.

- is promoted, leapfrogging over coworkers with more seniority
- wins a dream vacation to a place he detests
- with the help of chemical supplements, is now a voracious lover
- is profiled in a major magazine
- wins a spot on a reality television show
- gets a date with an unattainable somebody
- is the sole inheritor of a distant relative's large estate

Returning to Baseline

Something fortunate or unfortunate happens to your character. Will that experience fundamentally change him or will whatever change occurs last only a short while? Consider the interesting study conducted by experimental researchers P. Brickman, D. Coates, and R. Janoff-Bulman, who stated in "Lottery Winners and Accident Victims: Is Happiness Relative?" published in the *Journal of Personality and Social Psychology* that:

We studied both lottery winners and individuals who sustained a physical injury, to determine if winning the lottery made them happier or if sustaining an injury made them less happy. What we found was that immediately after either event, levels of happiness were higher (lottery winners), or lower (physically injured), and that after eight weeks or less, people returned to the level of happiness they had before the event.

Did You Know?

Here are some ups and downs in the lives of lottery winners as reported by researchers Guido W. Imbens, Donald B. Rubin, and Bruce Sacerdote in "Estimating the Effect of Unearned Income on Labor Supply, Earnings, Savings, and Consumption: Evidence From a Survey of Lottery Players," a study published in 2001 in *American Economic Review*:

- 88 percent still participate in the lottery every week
- 84 percent have not taken up any new hobbies since their win
- 75 percent now live in detached houses
- 56 percent who won more than $2,000,000 have given up work
- 48 percent are still in the same job
- 44 percent of their winnings were spent after five years
- 40 percent increased their contributions to charity
- 37 percent still buy supermarket brands
- 32 percent have gained weight since their win
- 19 percent went on holiday abroad for the first time
- 12 percent have joined health clubs
- 10 percent have switched to private medical coverage
- 3 percent moved their children from state schools to private schools

Food for Thought

- What are the psychological differences between an earned success (like tracking down a serial killer through painstaking investigative work) and a random success (like winning the lottery)?

- When can a success feel like a humiliation (for instance, winning an Academy Award after losing four different times and rightly feeling that the voters awarded you the Oscar out of pity)?

- What are the psychological differences between sudden success and gradual success (for instance, being handed a company to run versus running a company after thirty years of climbing the corporate ladder)?

SCENARIO NO. 29

BIG FAVOR

Your character's best friend asks her for a big favor—an enormous favor, really. Maybe the favor is that your character put up her friend's sister for a month. Maybe the favor is that your character use her contacts to land the friend a job. Maybe the favor is that your character lend her a sum of money. What big favor would it be interesting to investigate with respect to your character?

Get this big favor clearly in mind. Picture the circumstances of the announcement (is it in person, on the phone, by e-mail?), the style of the announcement (is it hesitant, aggressive, matter-of-fact?), the exact nature of the favor, and so on. Once you have this big favor in mind, proceed to the following questions.

1. Your character's best friend asks for a big favor. How does your character respond? Does she:

   A) Agree immediately and without hesitation?
   B) Agree immediately but reluctantly?
   C) Agree only after taking time to think the matter over?

D) Say no immediately?

E) Say no after thinking the matter over?

....

A) Agreeing immediately and without hesitation is consistent with a self-assured character who knows her own mind and makes snap decisions that she lives with happily or, alternatively, with a passive, pliable character who regularly says yes because she doesn't have the strength to say no.

B) Agreeing immediately but reluctantly is consistent with a dutiful character who prides herself on coming through in such situations but who really wishes that her friend hadn't asked for this particular favor.

C) Agreeing after taking time to think the matter over is consistent with a mature, responsible, likely optimistic character who knows the wisdom of reflecting before acting but who is inclined to stretch and take chances once she's given the matter its due consideration.

D) Saying no immediately is consistent with an oppositional, untrustworthy character who is more accustomed to taking than to giving or, alternatively, with a strong, forthright character who, in this set of circumstances, feels that she must say no and knows better than to delay delivering that unwelcome news.

E) Saying no after thinking the matter over is consistent with a conscientious, perhaps anxious and pessimistic character who is inclined to help but whose worries and fears outweigh her desire to be forthcoming.

How does your character respond to her best friend's request for a big favor?

2. Your character agrees to do the favor. How is she feeling?

A) Proud?

B) Irritated?

C) Anxious?

D) Excited?

E) Stoic?

....

A) Feeling proud is consistent with a principled character who holds helping a friend as one of her most cherished principles and who is likely as good as her word in all of her business and interpersonal dealings.

B) Feeling irritated is consistent with a conflicted character who feels torn between helping a friend and doubting the appropriateness of this favor and who is likely to regret agreeing should the favor prove especially difficult or produce any negative results.

C) Feeling anxious is consistent with a brooding character who regrets agreeing to help, both because of the possibility that she might fail and the possibility that her friend might fail her, for instance, by not repaying the loan.

D) Feeling excited is consistent with a bold, optimistic character who loves challenges, who is energized by helping, and who likely chose a profession that requires that she stretch and take risks.

E) Feeling stoic is consistent with a steady, hard-working character who feels it her duty to help, whether her heart is in helping or not, and who likely falls into the occasional depression by virtue of paying constant attention to her responsibilities at the expense of her dreams.

What does your character feel after agreeing to do her friend a big favor?

3. It turns out that doing the favor is much harder than she imagined it would be. Does she:

    A) Go the extra mile?
    B) Go back to her friend and co-create an alternative plan?
    C) Go back to her friend and back out?
    D) Make up a story and lie so as to get off the hook?
    E) Put the matter off and let it slip off her radar screen?

A) Going the extra mile is consistent with a disciplined, tough-minded character who may also be ambitious and even ruthless in the pursuit of her personal goals or, alternatively, with a proud, principled character who can be completely counted on in a pinch.

B) Going back to her friend and co-creating an alternative plan is consistent with a secure, self-confident character who understands that life is an intricate process with many ups and downs and that plans need tweaking and revising according to changed circumstances.

C) Going back to her friend and backing out is consistent with an insecure character who likely agreed because she felt she had to, was conflicted from the beginning, and was only waiting for some difficulty to arise so as to be able to save face and make her exit.

D) Making up a story and lying so as to get off the hook is consistent with a devious character who may have grown up in a household where the truth was in short supply, and who likely has addictive tendencies about which she also lies, saying, for instance, that she recently quit smoking when she has a pack of cigarettes right in her purse.

E) Putting the matter off and letting it slip off her radar screen is consistent with an anxious, defended character whose primary defense is denial and who likely lives a chaotic, disorganized, unfulfilled life because of the many important matters that, out of anxiety and defensiveness, she daily fails to address.

What would your character do if the favor turned out to be harder than she imagined it would be?

4. Your character successfully completes the favor. How does she react? Is she:

    A) Pleased?
    B) Indifferent?
    C) Jubilant?
    D) Relieved?
    E) Annoyed?

A) Feeling pleased is consistent with a secure, self-confident character who relishes success and who treats life in a straightforward manner, feeling good when things goes well without having to dilute her enjoyment or dismiss her accomplishments out of anxiety or defensiveness.

b) Feeling indifferent is consistent with a phlegmatic, philosophical character who is rarely roused to passion or, alternatively, with a depressed character who has lost the ability to feel pleasure.

c) Feeling jubilant is consistent with a manic, tightly wound character whose outsized reactions and extreme ups and downs make her unpredictable, crisis-prone, and ultimately unreliable.

d) Feeling relieved is consistent with an anxious character whose primary reaction to success of any sort is the release of the anxiety that had been building up as she worried about failing, followed almost immediately by the buildup of some new pressure, worry, and anxiety.

e) Feeling annoyed is consistent with a morose, pessimistic character who feels put upon and insufficiently recognized and rewarded, and who sees this not as a victory for friendship but as another instance of her being unfairly used and abused by the universe.

How would your character react to successfully completing the favor?

5. Your character reports her success to her friend and her friend fails to thank her. How does your character react?

    A) With compassion?
    B) With anger?
    c) With sadness?
    D) With annoyance?
    E) With amusement?

A) Reacting with compassion is consistent with an empathic character who recognizes when another person is under pressure or not in the right frame of mind to react appropriately and who prefers, as a matter of principle, to give people second chances and the benefit of the doubt.

B) Reacting with anger is consistent with a volatile, aggressive character who is quick to write off friends who fail her and who is probably tough-minded and litigious in her dealings with the world, standing ready to sue a neighbor or a business associate at the drop of a hat.

c) Reacting with sadness is consistent with a sensitive, depressed character who sees the world as a glass more than half-empty and who experiences human foibles as meaning drains that bring her closer to reckoning life completely pointless and worthless.

D) Reacting with annoyance is consistent with a secure, self-confident character who isn't inclined to blow her friend's failure all out of proportion but who also isn't inclined to let it pass unnoticed and who may therefore wonder aloud, "You don't seem very pleased that I'm loaning you this money. Why's that?"

E) Reacting with amusement is consistent with an ironic, educated, philo-sophical character who finds human beings lamentably ordinary and who actually enjoys having her low opinion of the human race confirmed by shortfalls of this sort.

How does your character react when her friend fails to thank her?

6. Your character has a big favor to ask of a friend (a different friend, let's say). Does she:

    A) Ask it reluctantly?
    B) Ask it matter-of-factly?
    C) Ask it demandingly?
    D) Ask it circumspectly?
    E) Not ask it?

A) Asking it reluctantly is consistent with a sensitive, empathic character who feels comfortable asking for favors but who also recognizes that favors come with a real cost to the other person and are likely to strain—and sometimes break—even sturdy friendships.

B) Asking it matter-of-factly is consistent with a self-assured character who takes it on principle that people should be treated as responsible adults capable of making decisions and that, therefore, not asking would only be a symptom of something like anxiety or squeamishness.

C) Asking it demandingly is consistent with an aggressive, perhaps abusive character whose interpersonal relationships are marked by fireworks and who likely has a childhood history of abuse and abandonment.

D) Asking it circumspectly is consistent with a passive-aggressive character who eschews directness and who is likely to feel anger and resentment toward her friend for not recognizing that a favor was requested, even though an observer would have to confess that he never heard the favor actually mentioned.

E) Not asking it is consistent with an anxious, insecure character who finds it difficult—and often impossible—to ask not only for big favors but for anything that she needs.

How does your character react to the prospect of asking a friend for a big favor?

Situations to Consider

What would your character do if:

- Another friend asked her to refuse the favor?
- She found the favor to be morally questionable?
- She knew that the favor would upset someone else?
- She suspected that her friend was making a mistake?
- She had already done her friend several big favors?
- Her friend had already done her several big favors?
- The favor required her telling a big lie?

Other Big Favor Situations

Put your character in the most appropriate of the following situations and think through how she would act and react. If you like, flesh out the scene by adding one conflict and one surprise.

- your character's boss asks her to do two jobs for an extended period of time as a favor
- your character's sixteen-year-old son asks to borrow the good car for a big date
- your character's sleazy cousin asks to come and live with her just until he gets on his feet
- your character's ex-boyfriend asks if he can leave his two parrots with her while he vacations in the Bahamas with his new girlfriend
- your character's younger sister asks her for a loan for a home down payment

- your character's best friend from high school, whom she hasn't seen in years, asks her to help her solve a family mystery
- your character's neighbor asks her to warn him if anybody comes looking for him

Why Do a Big Favor for a Friend?

Why would a person extend herself and do a friend a big favor? For one vital reason, if for no other reason: Friendship is so important to mental and physical health. Dr. Brian Gilmartin wrote in *Shyness & Love: Causes, Consequences, and Treatment*:

- Hospital patients who are married and who have friends who sincerely care about them recuperate from their surgical procedures significantly faster, and with fewer complications, than do those who are not married and/or do not have meaningful friendships.

- Elderly people whose rate of social interaction with friends is high tend to live significantly longer and enjoy significantly better health than do those elderly who do not enjoy meaningful friendships.

- In one study of pregnant women with many significant life changes, 91 percent of those whose family and friendship support was inadequate suffered birth complications, compared to only 33 percent of women who had the friendly support of family and friends.

- Alcoholics who try to stop drinking on their own are less than one-twentieth as likely to succeed as are those alcoholics who are well integrated into supportive family and friendship networks.

- Asthmatics who are poorly integrated into family and friendship support systems typically have to take as much as four times as much medication as those who enjoy the benefit of integration into such systems.

Did You Know?

Does having a good friend prevent mental illness? Gilmartin wrote:

In a random sample of women who had suffered a severe event or major difficulty in their lives, only 4 percent of those with a close confidante came down with a depressive psychiatric disorder, compared to 38 percent of those who did *not* have a confidante.

Food for Thought

• On average, is your character inclined to do favors for other people?

• On average, is your character inclined to accept favors from other people?

• Psychologically speaking, what is required to have a friend?

SCENARIO NO. 30
METEOR COMING

Scientists are almost certain that a meteor large enough to destroy the earth will strike in forty-eight hours. They can't say for sure where it will strike or what the consequences will be if it does strike, but those consequences are sure to range from the catastrophic to the apocalyptic.

Get this scenario clearly in mind. Is it a sunny day or a gloomy day? Is your character having a hectic afternoon or spending a quiet evening alone at home? How does he get the news—via an excited phone call or as he casually flips television channels? Once you have the setting, the time of day, and your character's frame of mind clearly in place, proceed to the following questions.

1. What is your character's first reaction to this news?

    A) Does your character panic?
    B) Is your character skeptical about the news?
    C) Does your character instantly begin to mobilize?
    D) Does your character rally his loved ones?
    E) Is your character indifferent to the news?

A) Reacting with panic is consistent with an anxious, overwrought character who habitually makes mountains out of molehills, casts every situation in its worst light, and likely is tormented by an array of phobias, from a phobic aversion to germs to a phobic fear of flying.

B) Receiving the news with skepticism is consistent with a thoughtful, educated character of the professional class who understands the speculative nature of scientific prediction and who has an intuitive sense of how long the odds must be that a meteor's path can be this accurately gauged.

C) Instantly beginning to mobilize is consistent with a resourceful, matter-of-fact character who likes to work with his hands, personally make repairs when things break, and who, whether a formal survivalist or not, has a survivalist's instincts for preparation and self-protection.

D) Rallying his loved ones is consistent with a mature, family-oriented character whose primary attachments are to family and friends, and who takes their well-being and protection as his primary responsibilities in life.

E) Reacting indifferently is consistent with a stoic, philosophical character who prides himself on his ability to take everything in stride, including the end of the world and his own death, or, alternatively, with a depressed character who has been forcing himself to live and who may anticipate the meteor's arrival as a godsend.

How does your character react to the news that life on earth may be ending in two days?

2. During that first day of waiting does your character:

    A) Go about his business as usual?
    B) Stay glued to his television set?
    C) Privately drink?
    D) Prepare to survive the impact?
    E) Prepare for the end?

A) Going about his business as usual is consistent with a stoic, phlegmatic character who prides himself on never getting his feathers ruffled or, alternatively, with a well-defended character who uses denial to mask his feelings of hysterical dread.

B) Staying glued to his television set is consistent with an anxious, social-ized and conventional character who follows every celebrity trial and pop commotion with great avidity, and whose sense of reality is largely formed by the mass media.

C) Privately drinking is consistent with a reclusive, antisocial character who is in the habit of binding anxiety with alcohol or, alternatively, with a melancholic, ironic character who feels it his duty to use up the good Scotch before the world ends.

D) Preparing to survive the impact is consistent with a tough-minded, as-sertive, self-reliant character who likely has been successful in business and knows how to take decisive action.

E) Preparing for the end is consistent with a character who was raised in a religious tradition that predicts the end of the world and who likely has an array of positive as well as fearful feelings about cataclysms and end time.

What does your character do during that first day of waiting?

3. There is a run on food. Does your character:

A) Rush out to the supermarket and stock up?
B) Watch news reports of the food riots with an ironic eye?
C) Watch news reports of the food riots with a fearful eye?
D) Go about his business?
E) Take his family out for a special dinner?

A) Rushing out to the supermarket to stock up is consistent with a panicked, hysterical character whose anxiety has gotten the better of him or, alter-natively, with an energetic, self-reliant character who intends to survive the meteor strike if there is any chance of surviving it.

B) Watching news reports of the food riots with an ironic eye is consistent with a thoughtful, educated character of the artistic or professional class who believes in the essential indifference of the universe to human affairs.

C) Watching news reports of the food riots with a fearful eye is a normal, unremarkable reaction and also consistent with a character who has experienced a trauma like a famine or a great depression and who knows firsthand the horrors and barbarities that can accompany a society-wide cataclysm.

D) Going about his business is consistent with a frightened character who is binding his anxiety by obsessively going through the motions or, alternatively, with a stoic character who has endured many hardships and disappointments in life and prefers to mind his own business and put one foot in front of the other.

E) Taking his family out for a special dinner is consistent with a stoic, philosophical character who presumes that a good dinner with his family will serve both as a poignant last celebration and an absurd tip-of-the-hat to fate.

What would your character do if there were a run on food?

4. The president appears on television to calm the populace and to outline what people should do in this emergency. Does your character:

   A) Obediently follow the president's plan?
   B) Follow the president's plan, but only if it makes sense to him?
   c) Debate the merits of the president's plan with friends and acquaintances?
   D) Dismiss the president's plan as some kind of government scam?
   E) Take no notice of the address or the plan?

A) Obediently following the president's plan is consistent with a conventional, socialized character whose primary goals in life are to fit in and not make waves and who will criticize—perhaps unmercifully—anyone who dares to think for himself.

B) Following the president's plan, but only if makes sense to him, is consistent with a thoughtful, self-confident, educated character who is skeptical of government pronouncements and who prides himself on making up his own mind on matters of any significance.

c) Debating the merits of the plan with friends and acquaintances is consistent with a garrulous, oppositional character who likes to play devil's advocate just to rile people or, alternatively, with a lonely character who uses current events to make contact with other human beings.

D) Dismissing the president's plan as some kind of government scam is consistent with a grandiose, paranoid character whose anxiety manifests as suspiciousness or, alternatively, with a sensibly skeptical character who knows history and is alert to the ways that politicians lie and manipulate.

E) Taking no notice of the address or the plan is consistent with a reclusive character lost in his own world or, alternatively, with a stoic, philosophical character who has decided to let fate dictate what the next forty-eight hours will bring.

What would your character do if the president offered the nation a plan to deal with this emergency?

5. The meteor is due to arrive (or pass by) in the next fifteen minutes. What does your character do?

    A) Watch the news coverage?
    B) Drink heavily?
    C) Make love?
    D) Act as if nothing is happening?
    E) Go outside to await the impact?

A) Watching the news coverage is consistent with a passive, conventional, socialized character who finds himself treating this more as a media event than an actual crisis and who experiences himself as an observer rather than an actor in life.

B) Drinking heavily is consistent with an anxious character with addictive tendencies who binds his anxiety with alcohol and who binge drinks in especially stressful situations.

C) Making love is consistent with a strong, passionate, life-loving character who would really prefer not to die and who means to extract the last measure of love and intimacy out of what may be his and his lover's last moments on earth.

D) Acting as if nothing is happening is consistent with a stoic character who intends to thumb his nose at the gods or, alternatively, with a heavily defended character engaged in denial who would dissolve into hysteria if his defenses failed him.

E) Going outside to await the impact is consistent with an aggressive, oppositional character who is used to brawling and flexing his muscles and who would punch the meteor in the nose if that were possible.

What would your character do in the minutes leading up to the arrival of the meteor?

6. The meteor passes the earth by. How does your character react?

    A) Opens the best Scotch?
    B) Falls asleep out of tense exhaustion?
    C) Hugs his mate and children?
    D) Rails at the scientists for their scare tactics and misinformation?
    E) Begins worrying about something new?

A) Opening the best Scotch is consistent with a passionate, powerful character who knows when a celebration is deserved and who may continue celebrating in small and large ways for weeks to come.

B) Falling asleep out of tense exhaustion is consistent with an emotionally fragile character who was likely already stressed out before this crisis commenced and who has reached his stress saturation level.

C) Hugging his mate and children is consistent with a life-loving, empathic character who values his relationships above all else and who may discover that what he most wants next is a family vacation, to honor and celebrate their mutual survival.

D) Railing at the scientists is consistent with an angry, oppositional, pessimistic character who finds it impossible to take pleasure in life and whose reaction to having his life spared is to search for someone to blame for inconveniencing him.

E) Beginning to worry about something new is consistent with an anxious character whose pattern is to move seamlessly from worry to worry and who regularly inclines toward depression.

How does your character react to the earth's being spared?

Situations to Consider

What would your character do if:

- Someone tried to break in to steal your character's food?

- An acquaintance asked to share your character's storm cellar?

- Your character's young child asked where we go after we die?

- A close friend became hysterical?

- The police ordered everyone to stay indoors?

- An acquaintance offered to sell your character firearms for after the apocalypse?

- The meteor struck and produced, not the end of the world, but widespread destruction?

Other Apocalyptic Situations

Put your character in the most appropriate of the following situations and think through how he would act and react. If you like, flesh out the scene by adding one conflict and one surprise.

- a highly contagious plague strikes
- a tsunami is predicted
- two nuclear nations look poised to launch their missiles
- the ozone layer is suddenly dramatically degraded
- an endless drought leads to famine
- during a war, the enemy army approaches
- civil war erupts after a long economic depression

Apocalyptic and Post-Apocalyptic Fiction

If this scenario appealed to you, you may have a taste for apocalyptic literature. Here are ten classics of the genre.

- *Lucifer's Hammer*, by Larry Niven and Jerry Pournelle. Giant comet slams into earth, unleashing killer earthquakes and tidal waves and setting the stage for man's struggle for survival as a new Ice Age dawns.

- *On the Beach*, by Nevil Shute. Classic story of Aussies waiting for the radiation cloud unleashed by nuclear war to reach them.

- *Alas, Babylon*, by Pat Frank. People in a small Florida town cope with the events leading up to, and the consequences of, nuclear war.

- *Last Ship*, by William Brinkley. Global nuclear disaster has struck and the guided-missile destroyer *Nathan James*, short on food and fuel, its crew of men and women seriously depleted by desertions, sails the seas in search of an uncontaminated landfall.

- *Earth Abides*, by George R. Stewart. A disease of unparalleled destructive force has sprung up, all but destroying the human race. One survivor, strangely immune to the effects of the epidemic, ventures forward to experience a world without man.

- *The Stand*, by Stephen King. A rapidly mutating flu virus is accidentally released from a U.S. military facility and wipes out most of the world's population, setting the stage for an apocalyptic confrontation between good and evil.

- *This Is the Way the Earth Ends*, by James Morrow. In this novel of nuclear holocaust, six survivors representing mankind are tried by an alien prosecutor for their complicity in the war.

- *The Postman*, by David Brin. A survivor of the Doomsday war spends years crossing a post-apocalypse United States looking for something to believe in, finally finding it in the made-up role of a "Restored United States" postal inspector.

- *Riddley Walker*, by Russell Hoban. Written in post-apocalyptic slang, a tale of human beings surviving a Dark Age long after a nuclear war has struck.

- *Eternity Road*, by Jack McDevitt. Set a thousand years from now, when the world as we know it has been dead for eight centuries, destroyed by a cataclysmic viral plague that killed most of humanity.

Did You Know?

Natural disaster coupled with a fear of future disaster can lead to mass hysteria. Richard Owen reported the following in an article titled "Quaking Italians Fear the Apocalypse Now," which appeared in the *London Times* in October 1997:

Another powerful tremor hit Umbria yesterday, as rumors spread throughout Italy that "the Big One" would strike today, in accordance with the prophecies of Nostradamus. ... "An earthquake obsession without end" was the head-line in yesterday's *La Stampa*, which reported that people near the epicenter were "awaiting the end of the world." Psychologists said pre-millennial fears were becoming widespread and the continuing quakes were giving rise to a national psychosis.

How will your character react if all around him people are losing their heads?

Food for Thought

• How does your character view death?

• How barbarous could your character become, given an apocalyptic calamity?

• Would your character lead or follow after an apocalypse?

CHARACTER PSYCHOLOGY
IN SHORT STORIES

RECOMMENDED READING

Many of the scenarios presented in this book are not uncommon in fiction. The short stories listed below contain themes and scenes that link to some of the scenarios suggested in this book. You might find reading a few of these useful as you work with your characters. One source for each short story is listed; however, many of these stories have been published in other anthologies and some were first published in magazines. The numbers in parentheses indicate the scenarios with which the stories are linked.

"A & P," by John Updike in *Literature: An Introduction to Fiction, Poetry, and Drama, 9th edition* **(7)**

"A Good Man Is Hard to Find," by Flannery O'Connor in *The Complete Stories* **(15, 4)**

"A Jury of Her Peers," by Susan Glaspell in *A Jury of Her Peers: Short Stories* **(2)**

"A Pair of Tickets," by Amy Tan in *Literature: An Introduction to Fiction, Poetry, and Drama, 9th edition* **(8)**

"A Rose for Emily," by William Faulkner *Collected Stories of William Faulkner* **(17)**

"Barn Burning," by William Faulkner in *Collected Stories of William Faulkner* **(21, 22)**

"Blueprints," by Barbara Kingsolver in *Homeland and Other Stories* **(27)**

"Brothers and Sisters Around the World," by Andrea Lee *Best American Short Stories 2001* **(7)**

"Bullet in the Brain," by Tobias Wolff in *Seven Hundred Kisses* **(20)**

"Chrysanthemums," by John Steinbeck in *Literature: An Introduction to Fiction, Poetry, and Drama, 9th edition* **(6)**

"Devotion," by Adam Haslett in *Best American Short Stories 2003* **(24)**

"Fender Bender," by Simon Wood in *Small Crimes* **(4)**

"Games," by Katherine MacLean in *Nebula Awards Showcase 2004* **(13)**

"Good Country People," by Flannery O'Connor in *The Complete Stories* **(6)**

"Greasy Lake," by T. Coraghessan Boyle in *Literature: An Introduction to Fiction, Poetry, and Drama, 9th edition* **(21)**

"Harrison Bergeron," by Kurt Vonnegut in *Welcome to the Monkey House* **(12)**

"His," by Carolyn Banks in *Seven Hundred Kisses* **(18)**

"I Stand Here Ironing," by Tillie Olsen in *Literature: An Introduction to Fiction, Poetry and Drama, 9th edition* **(14)**

"Jump-up Day," by Barbara Kingsolver in *Homeland and Other Stories* **(25)**

"Mirror Studies," by Mary Yukari Waters in *Best American Short Stories 2004* **(23)**

"Miss Brill," by Katherine Mansfield in *Perrine's Story and Structure, 11th edition* **(14)**

"My Father's Secret," by Nguyen Quang Thieu in *Love After War: Contemporary Fiction From Vietnam* **(24, 25)**

"My Life With the Wave," by Octavio Paz in *Harper Anthology of Fiction* **(18)**

"Nothing Ever Happens in Rock City," by Jack McDevitt in *Nebula Awards Showcase 2004* **(9)**

"Paul's Case," by Willa Cather in *The Troll Garden: Short Stories* **(20, 24)**

"Stalking," by Joyce Carol Oates in *Marriages and Infidelities* **(18)**

"The Garden Party," by Katherine Mansfield in *The Garden Party, and Other Stories* **(5)**

"The Japanese Quince," by John Galsworthy in *Perrine's Story and Structure, 11th edition* **(14)**

"The Jilting of Granny Weatherall," by Katherine Anne Porter in *The Collected Stories of Katherine Anne Porter* **(25)**

"The Most Dangerous Game," by Richard Connell in *Perrine's Story and Structure, 11th edition* **(18)**

"The Necklace," by Guy de Maupassant in *The Necklace and Other Short Stories* **(24)**

"The Raft," by Peter Orner in *Best American Short Stories 2001* **(22, 24)**

"To Da-duh, In Memoriam," by Paule Marshall in *The Heath Anthology of American Literature, 5th edition* **(15)**

"What Means Switch," by Gish Jen in *Growing Up Ethnic in America* **(9)**

"Where Are You Going, Where Have You Been?" by Joyce Carol Oates in *Where Are You Going, Where Have You Been?: Stories* **(20, 21, 18)**

"Written in Stone," by Catherine Brady in *Best American Short Stories 2004* **(27)**

"Young Goodman Brown," by Nathanial Hawthorne in *Literature: An Introduction to Fiction, Poetry, and Drama* **(13)**

INDEX

About the Authors

ERIC MAISEL, PH.D., is a licensed family therapist, creativity coach, and creativity coach trainer with a doctorate in counseling psychology and master's degrees in creative writing and counseling. His more than twenty-five works of nonfiction and fiction include *The Van Gogh Blues*, a Books for a Better Life Award finalist; *Affirmations for Artists*, named best book of the year for artists by *New Age Magazine*; *Fearless Creating*; *The Creativity Book*; and the recently published *Coaching the Artist Within*, *A Writer's Paris*, and *The Ten Second Pause*.

A regular contributor to *Writer's Digest* magazine and *The Writer* magazine, Maisel writes a monthly "Coaching the Artist Within" column for *Art Calendar* magazine and founded and wrote *Callboard* magazine's "Staying Sane in the Theater" column. Regarded as America's foremost creativity coach, Maisel maintains a private creativity coaching practice in San Francisco, facilitates the Creativity Coaching Certification Program for the Institute of Transpersonal Psychology, and trains creativity coaches nationally and internationally.

You can learn more about Dr. Maisel's books and creativity coaching services at www.ericmaisel.com, and you can contact him at ericmaisel@hotmail.com.

ANN MAISEL, M.A., taught world literature for twenty-five years. She currently serves as associate head of Lick-Wilmerding High School in San Francisco.